MySQL Mastery: From Basics to Brilliance – A Journey Through SQL and Beyond

Table of Contents

This Table of Contents guides readers from the fundamentals of MySQL to more advanced topics, ensuring a smooth and structured learning experience from novice to expert.

Chapter 1: Introduction to MySQL: Your First Step Toward Mastery

1. MySQL is one of the most popular relational database management systems (RDBMS) used around the world today. Whether you are building a website, managing business data, or working on a software development project, understanding how MySQL works is essential. This chapter will guide you through the basics of MySQL, introducing the system, its features, and why it's a great choice for beginners. You'll learn the fundamental concepts behind databases, how MySQL fits into the larger database ecosystem, and why it remains one of the most reliable tools for managing data. MySQL allows you to create, modify, and query databases through SQL, which stands for Structured Query Language. SQL is the language used to interact with the database, and understanding it is critical to unlocking the power of MySQL. By the end of this chapter, you'll have a clear understanding of MySQL and how it will serve as the foundation for your journey toward mastery.

2. Before diving into MySQL itself, it's helpful to understand what a database is. A database is simply an organized collection of data. In MySQL, data is stored in tables, with rows representing records and columns representing attributes of those records. Think of a table as a spreadsheet where each row contains information about an entity, such as a customer, product, or order. Each column in the table holds specific information about the entity, like name, price, or address. These tables work together to form a larger database, which can hold millions of records. Understanding this structure is important, as it helps you visualize how data is organized and accessed in MySQL. The relational model, which is what MySQL uses, organizes data into tables that can be linked together through relationships, making it highly effective for managing complex datasets.

3. One of the key benefits of MySQL is its simplicity and ease of use. Whether you're a complete beginner or an experienced developer, you'll find MySQL approachable. The software has an intuitive interface and powerful query capabilities that allow you to manipulate data with ease. You don't need to be an expert in databases to start using

MySQL, as its syntax is straightforward and user-friendly. Over time, as you grow more experienced, you can explore advanced features like joins, indexes, and stored procedures. But first, it's important to understand the core components of MySQL, and this chapter will break those down for you. You will also learn about how MySQL interacts with SQL to carry out tasks such as querying, updating, and deleting data.

4. MySQL has been around for over two decades and is developed by Oracle Corporation, though it remains open-source, meaning anyone can use and modify it for free. This open-source nature has contributed significantly to MySQL's popularity, as developers around the world continue to improve and adapt it to meet various needs. Many large-scale organizations, including tech giants like Facebook, Google, and Twitter, use MySQL for handling massive volumes of data. Despite its robust feature set, MySQL is lightweight and fast, making it ideal for applications with high performance demands. It's this combination of power, flexibility, and speed that makes MySQL an attractive option for both small businesses and large enterprises. As you continue your journey with MySQL, you'll see how it has evolved over the years to become one of the most reliable and widely used database systems.

5. The MySQL community is vast, with millions of users and contributors sharing knowledge, troubleshooting issues, and improving the software. This community-driven approach means there's always a wealth of resources available, whether through official documentation, forums, or tutorials. As a beginner, you will find numerous guides and examples to help you get started with MySQL. And, as you progress, you'll be able to access deeper levels of support for more advanced techniques. The MySQL ecosystem also includes various tools that can help with database design, management, and performance optimization. From graphical user interfaces (GUIs) like MySQL Workbench to command-line tools, there are plenty of options for interacting with MySQL databases.

6. In terms of popularity, MySQL ranks as one of the top choices for web developers, especially in combination with other technologies like PHP and JavaScript. Together, these technologies make up the "LAMP" stack (Linux, Apache, MySQL, PHP), a popular framework for building web applications. If you are planning to develop websites or web applications, learning MySQL will be an essential part of your skill set. Even outside of web development, MySQL is used in industries such as finance, healthcare, and e-commerce, where data management is critical. The scalability and flexibility of MySQL make it a reliable solution for handling data in various environments. As you continue through this book, you'll learn how MySQL powers some of the biggest and most complex systems in the world.

7. MySQL is compatible with a wide range of operating systems, including Linux, Windows, and macOS. This cross-platform capability ensures that MySQL can be used in many different environments, whether you're working on a personal laptop or managing enterprise-level systems. The installation process is simple, and once you have it set up, you'll be able to create and manage your own databases with ease. MySQL offers both command-line and graphical user interfaces (GUIs) for interacting with databases, so you

can choose whichever method feels most comfortable. As a beginner, it's recommended to start with the GUI tools, as they provide a more user-friendly experience.

8. One of the most important concepts to understand when working with MySQL is SQL, or Structured Query Language. SQL is the language used to communicate with databases, and it allows you to query, modify, and manage data. MySQL uses SQL to carry out its operations, so understanding SQL is crucial for mastering MySQL. In this book, we'll guide you through the syntax and structure of SQL, covering essential commands like SELECT, INSERT, UPDATE, and DELETE. By mastering these commands, you'll be able to perform tasks like retrieving data from tables, adding new data, updating existing data, and deleting unnecessary data. SQL is a powerful language, and with a little practice, you'll be able to write complex queries that retrieve exactly the information you need.

9. At the core of MySQL is the relational model, which is based on the idea of organizing data into tables. Each table in MySQL consists of rows and columns, with each row representing a unique record and each column representing an attribute of that record. For example, in a "Customers" table, each row might represent a different customer, and the columns would store attributes like the customer's name, email, and address. By organizing data in this way, MySQL makes it easy to manage and query large amounts of information. You'll learn how to design and structure your own tables throughout this book, enabling you to build efficient and effective databases.

10. MySQL is built around the concept of relational data, which means that tables can be related to one another. These relationships allow data to be connected across multiple tables, making it possible to query and retrieve information from different sources. One of the key tools for establishing relationships between tables is the use of keys. Primary keys uniquely identify each record in a table, while foreign keys establish a connection between tables. By understanding these relationships, you'll be able to create more complex and efficient queries that can pull data from multiple tables at once.

11. In addition to basic data storage and retrieval, MySQL also provides powerful tools for managing and securing your data. You'll learn how to implement constraints to ensure data integrity, such as setting fields to be unique or not allowing NULL values. MySQL also allows you to create indexes, which improve the speed and efficiency of queries by allowing faster searches through large datasets. Advanced features like stored procedures, triggers, and views allow you to automate processes and simplify your database management. As you move through the chapters of this book, you'll explore these features and how they can be used to enhance your work with MySQL.

12. Another important aspect of MySQL is its ability to scale. Whether you're working with a small personal project or an enterprise-level application, MySQL is capable of handling databases of all sizes. The system can be fine-tuned for performance through various configuration options, and there are tools available to monitor and optimize its performance. As your database grows, MySQL can be scaled to meet the increasing demands of your project. You'll learn how to manage large databases and optimize

queries for speed and efficiency, ensuring that your applications remain fast and responsive.

13. MySQL supports the use of transactions, which allow you to group multiple operations together into a single, atomic unit. Transactions are essential for ensuring data consistency and integrity, especially in scenarios where multiple users are accessing and modifying the same data simultaneously. In a transaction, changes are not committed to the database until all operations are successfully completed, ensuring that your data remains consistent. You'll learn how to use transaction commands like COMMIT, ROLLBACK, and SAVEPOINT to control how changes are made to your database and prevent errors from affecting your data.

14. As you become more familiar with MySQL, you'll also learn how to perform more advanced tasks, such as database backups and replication. Backing up your data is critical for protecting it from accidental loss or corruption, and MySQL provides a variety of methods for creating backups. Replication allows you to create copies of your database across multiple servers, improving availability and performance. By the end of this book, you'll understand how to implement these features and ensure that your data remains safe and accessible.

15. MySQL is a versatile and flexible tool that can be used in a variety of settings. From personal projects to large-scale enterprise systems, MySQL is capable of handling the demands of any application. Its combination of speed, power, and ease of use makes it a go-to choice for developers around the world. As you continue through this book, you'll discover the many ways that MySQL can be leveraged to build effective and efficient database systems.

16. One of the most exciting aspects of MySQL is its ability to integrate with other programming languages. For example, MySQL can be used in conjunction with PHP, Python, and JavaScript, allowing you to create dynamic websites and web applications. By learning how MySQL integrates with these languages, you'll be able to build full-fledged applications that use MySQL as the backend database. You'll also explore how to use MySQL with frameworks like Node.js and Django, expanding your ability to work on modern web development projects.

As you dive deeper into MySQL, you'll also encounter topics like data normalization, indexing, and query optimization. These concepts will help you design more efficient and scalable databases. Data normalization is the process of organizing data to reduce redundancy and improve consistency. Essentially, it’s about ensuring that each piece of information is stored in only one place, reducing the chances of errors and making updates easier. Indexing, on the other hand, is the creation of pointers that allow MySQL to quickly locate specific rows in a table, speeding up query execution times. This is particularly important for large databases where searches might otherwise take a long time. Query optimization focuses on writing efficient queries that minimize the load on the database and reduce processing time. This includes understanding how to structure queries for faster results, how to use appropriate indexes, and how to analyze execution plans to spot bottlenecks. Mastering these advanced techniques will help you work with large, complex data sets more effectively and ensure that your MySQL databases perform at their best.

Throughout this book, you'll be guided step-by-step through the process of becoming proficient with MySQL. Whether you're a complete beginner or someone with some experience in databases, you'll find this book easy to follow and packed with useful information. Each chapter builds on the previous one, gradually introducing more complex concepts and features. We'll start with simple database operations and work our way toward advanced topics such as optimizing database performance and implementing complex joins. The goal is to ensure that you build a solid foundation in MySQL and understand not only how to perform basic tasks but also how to approach database design and optimization with confidence. Along the way, you'll find plenty of examples and practice exercises to help reinforce your learning. With patience and persistence, you'll be able to take on real-world MySQL challenges and solve them effectively.

It's important to note that MySQL is not just for developers – it's also widely used by system administrators, data analysts, and business intelligence professionals. These users rely on MySQL to manage and analyze data, generate reports, and make data-driven decisions. Whether you're working in IT, marketing, sales, or any field that involves handling large amounts of data, MySQL is a crucial tool for managing and understanding that information. For system administrators, MySQL can be used to configure and maintain the database servers that power websites, applications, and internal systems. Data analysts and business intelligence professionals use MySQL to query large datasets, run complex analytics, and extract meaningful insights from raw data. If you're interested in working with data at a professional level, learning MySQL is an essential skill. This book will provide you with the foundation you need to succeed in any role that involves working with data, whether it's building databases from scratch or analyzing existing ones.

In conclusion, MySQL is a powerful and versatile database system that is essential for anyone working with data. Whether you're building websites, managing business data, or developing software applications, MySQL will be a key tool in your arsenal. Its flexibility and ease of use make it a great choice for beginners, while its advanced features and performance capabilities ensure it remains relevant in even the most demanding environments. Throughout this book, you'll gain the knowledge and experience needed to master MySQL, from basic queries to advanced features like joins, indexing, and replication. By the end of this journey, you'll be well-equipped to tackle any database challenge and unlock the full potential of MySQL. As you continue, remember that mastery comes with practice, so take your time with the exercises and concepts presented. Let's get started with your first step toward mastery – we're about to dive into creating your first database and running your first query!

Chapter 2: Setting Up Your MySQL Environment

1. Setting up MySQL is the first practical step on your journey toward becoming proficient in database management. While it's possible to use MySQL without a local installation by leveraging cloud databases, setting up MySQL on your own computer or server offers a hands-on experience and provides greater flexibility. This chapter will guide you through the installation and configuration process for MySQL on various platforms, including Windows, macOS, and Linux. Before diving into using MySQL, it's important to make

sure that your environment is correctly set up. We'll walk through the steps needed to install MySQL, configure the system, and troubleshoot common installation issues. Once you've successfully set up MySQL, you'll be ready to start creating databases and running SQL queries. Let's begin by looking at the basic steps to get MySQL up and running on your machine.

2. MySQL can be installed on different operating systems, each with its own set of requirements and procedures. If you're using Windows, MySQL offers a handy installer that simplifies the installation process. This installer includes everything you need to run MySQL on Windows, including the MySQL Server, Workbench, and other tools. On macOS, MySQL can be installed via Homebrew or by downloading a native installer from the MySQL website. If you're working with Linux, the process can vary depending on your distribution, but most Linux systems support MySQL installation through package managers like APT (for Ubuntu) or YUM (for CentOS). In all cases, the MySQL website provides detailed, up-to-date instructions for each platform, and we'll cover some of these installation methods in detail as well.

3. The first step in installing MySQL is downloading the appropriate installer for your system. Go to the official MySQL website (https://dev.mysql.com/downloads/) and select the MySQL Community Edition, which is free to use. For Windows, you can choose the MySQL Installer, which provides a GUI to help guide you through the process. For macOS and Linux, you'll be downloading the MySQL server package, which includes both the database server and client programs. Once the installer is downloaded, you can start the installation process. Be sure to check for any additional requirements or dependencies, as some systems may require specific versions of software libraries or tools. If you're using a package manager on Linux, you'll be using commands like `sudo apt-get install mysql-server` or `sudo yum install mysql-server` to install the necessary packages.

4. After downloading the installer, the next step is to launch it and follow the on-screen instructions. On Windows, the MySQL Installer provides a user-friendly interface that guides you through selecting features, setting up your MySQL server, and choosing installation options. One of the key decisions you'll make during installation is selecting a root password for MySQL. This password is important because it grants you administrative privileges for managing the database server. It's crucial to choose a strong and secure password to prevent unauthorized access to your databases. Similarly, on macOS and Linux, the installation process will guide you through configuring the server, setting up a root password, and configuring networking options.

5. Once the installation is complete, you'll need to configure MySQL to ensure it runs properly on your system. On Windows, this often involves configuring MySQL as a service that will start automatically when your computer boots up. During installation, the MySQL Installer typically handles this configuration for you, but you can also manually adjust the service settings later if necessary. On macOS and Linux, MySQL is typically installed as a service by default, but you'll need to ensure that the MySQL service is started and enabled to run automatically. You can do this by running commands like

`sudo systemctl start mysql` and `sudo systemctl enable mysql` on Linux. Once MySQL is running, you should be able to connect to the server through a terminal or MySQL Workbench, depending on your preference.

6. After configuring MySQL, you can test that the installation was successful by connecting to the MySQL server. On Windows, you can use MySQL Workbench or the command line to connect to the server. MySQL Workbench provides a graphical interface that allows you to execute queries, manage databases, and visualize your data. For the command line, you can open a terminal and type `mysql -u root -p`, followed by your root password. If everything is set up correctly, you'll be logged into the MySQL command-line interface (CLI), where you can start issuing SQL commands. On macOS and Linux, the process is similar, and you can use the terminal to connect to MySQL. Once logged in, you should see the MySQL prompt, indicating that your installation is working as expected.

7. If you run into any issues during the installation process, there are several troubleshooting steps you can take. For Windows, make sure that you've installed any required dependencies and that your system meets the minimum hardware requirements. If MySQL fails to start, it could be due to conflicts with other software or a misconfiguration during the installation process. Checking the MySQL error log can often reveal the cause of the issue. On macOS and Linux, make sure that your system is up to date and that you're using the correct installation method for your distribution. If MySQL is not starting, you can check the status of the MySQL service using the command `sudo systemctl status mysql` on Linux. For both macOS and Linux, be aware that you might need to configure your firewall to allow MySQL connections, especially if you're working in a multi-user environment.

8. Once MySQL is successfully installed and running, it's time to explore the configuration files. These files control various settings, such as memory allocation, connection limits, and buffer sizes. In most cases, the default configuration will work fine for beginners, but as you progress, you may need to tweak these settings for better performance. On Windows, MySQL configuration files are typically located in the `MySQL Server` directory. On Linux and macOS, the main configuration file is usually located at `/etc/my.cnf` or `/etc/mysql/my.cnf`. Understanding these configuration files and making adjustments can help optimize your MySQL environment for specific use cases, such as large-scale applications or high-traffic websites.

9. MySQL also offers several command-line tools that make managing your databases easier. The `mysqladmin` command is used for administrative tasks such as checking server status, creating databases, or restarting MySQL. You can also use the `mysqldump` tool to back up your databases and the `mysqlimport` tool for importing data. These tools are invaluable when managing MySQL servers in production environments or when automating database management tasks. MySQL Workbench, a GUI tool, provides an even more user-friendly experience for creating, modifying, and querying databases. Workbench also includes a visual query builder, which can help

beginners understand how SQL queries are constructed without needing to memorize all the syntax.

10. In addition to MySQL Workbench, there are other third-party tools available for managing MySQL. phpMyAdmin is a popular web-based tool that provides a graphical interface for interacting with MySQL databases. It’s commonly used in shared hosting environments and by developers who prefer a web interface. Navicat and HeidiSQL are two other third-party tools that provide a rich set of features for managing MySQL databases. While MySQL Workbench is great for beginners, exploring these other tools can give you more options and flexibility as you become more familiar with MySQL.

11. Once MySQL is installed and configured, it’s time to start creating your first databases. The first step in database creation is deciding what kind of information you want to store. For example, if you're building a website, you might create databases for users, products, and orders. In MySQL, creating a database is as simple as typing `CREATE DATABASE` followed by the name of your database. After creating a database, you can create tables within that database to store your data. Each table consists of columns, and each column holds a specific type of data, such as numbers, text, or dates. You’ll learn how to create and modify tables in subsequent chapters.

12. As you begin to work with MySQL, it’s important to set up a secure environment. Even if you're working on a local machine, security should be a priority, especially if you’re going to expose MySQL to the internet or multiple users. The first step is securing your root account by using a strong password, which you should have done during installation. Next, you should limit MySQL’s access by configuring your firewall and user privileges. MySQL allows you to assign different levels of permissions to different users, such as read-only access or full administrative privileges. You can also configure MySQL to only allow connections from specific IP addresses or hostnames, which helps prevent unauthorized access.

13. Another key security practice is regularly updating MySQL to patch any security vulnerabilities. MySQL is actively maintained, and updates often include fixes for known security issues. Whether you are using Windows, macOS, or Linux, make sure to check for MySQL updates regularly. On Linux, package managers like APT or YUM can be used to check for and install updates. For Windows, MySQL provides an installer that can be run to check for updates. It's also a good idea to review MySQL's security documentation periodically, as the software is continually evolving to meet new security challenges.

14. Backup and recovery are two of the most important tasks you’ll perform as a MySQL administrator. It’s essential to regularly back up your databases to avoid data loss due to hardware failure, accidental deletion, or other unforeseen issues. MySQL offers several ways to back up your databases, including using the `mysqldump` command-line tool or by setting up scheduled backups with cron jobs on Linux. For more advanced setups, you can implement replication to create copies of your data on other servers. In the event of a failure, you'll need to restore your data from backups. Understanding how to back up and

restore your databases will be critical to ensuring the reliability of your MySQL environment.

15. To ensure that MySQL runs efficiently, you'll need to monitor its performance regularly. Tools like `MySQL Enterprise Monitor` or `Percona Monitoring and Management` can help you track server health, query performance, and overall system resource usage. As you work with larger datasets and more complex queries, monitoring becomes increasingly important. You can also use the `SHOW STATUS` command within MySQL to view real-time information about server performance. This includes details about connections, query execution times, and memory usage. By regularly monitoring your MySQL environment, you can identify potential issues before they impact performance.

16. As you continue to explore MySQL, it's a good idea to familiarize yourself with some of the advanced configuration options available. For example, MySQL allows you to tune memory settings to optimize performance for your specific workload. The `innodb_buffer_pool_size` setting controls how much memory is allocated to caching data and indexes, which can significantly impact query speed. Similarly, the `max_connections` setting controls how many simultaneous client connections MySQL can handle. Tuning these parameters can make your database perform much better, especially in high-traffic scenarios.

17. In this chapter, we've covered the installation and initial configuration of MySQL on multiple platforms. Now that your environment is set up, you're ready to start interacting with MySQL and exploring its features in more depth. The next chapter will guide you through basic SQL queries, showing you how to retrieve and manipulate data within your new MySQL database. Before moving forward, take some time to explore the MySQL interface and ensure you're comfortable navigating the various tools. The more familiar you become with MySQL's interface and configuration options, the more effective you will be at managing databases in the future.

18. As a beginner, the most important takeaway from this chapter is that a solid setup is the foundation for successful database management. Without a properly configured MySQL environment, working with databases would be much more difficult. Now that you've installed MySQL and configured it to your needs, you're ready to begin creating databases, writing SQL queries, and building robust database applications. Whether you're using MySQL for a personal project, a web application, or in a professional setting, understanding how to properly set up and maintain your MySQL environment is key to success.

19. If you encounter any issues during the installation or configuration process, remember that the MySQL community is vast, and there are plenty of resources available to help you troubleshoot. From forums to official documentation, you'll find assistance from other users and developers who have faced similar challenges. Don't hesitate to seek help when needed, as understanding and solving these issues will only strengthen your knowledge of MySQL.

20. With MySQL now set up and configured, you've completed a crucial step toward becoming proficient with databases. In the next chapter, we'll dive into the basics of MySQL queries, starting with how to retrieve and filter data. You'll begin learning the powerful SQL commands that allow you to interact with your database and manipulate the data within. By the end of this book, you'll be able to build complex databases, optimize their performance, and secure your data, ensuring you're fully prepared for any database-related challenge you encounter.

Chapter 3: Getting Started with MySQL: Understanding Basic Queries

1. Now that you've successfully set up MySQL, it's time to start working with it! The first step in using MySQL is understanding how to write and execute basic queries. SQL (Structured Query Language) is the language used to interact with MySQL, and it allows you to create, read, update, and delete data in your databases. In this chapter, we'll explore the basics of writing SQL queries, focusing on the most common and fundamental commands. We'll start with the SELECT statement, which is used to retrieve data from a database. Understanding how to query and retrieve information is crucial for working with MySQL, and it's the foundation for more complex queries. By the end of this chapter, you'll be comfortable writing your first SQL queries and extracting meaningful data from your databases.

2. A SQL query is essentially a request for data from a MySQL database. The SELECT statement is the core of most SQL queries because it allows you to retrieve data from one or more tables. The syntax of a basic SELECT query is simple: you begin with the keyword `SELECT`, followed by the column names you want to retrieve, and then specify the table from which to retrieve the data. For example, if you have a table called `customers` and you want to retrieve the customer names, the query would look like this: `SELECT name FROM customers;`. This will return all the names from the `customers` table. Notice that the query starts with `SELECT`, followed by the column name (`name`), and then the table name (`customers`). This is the basic structure of a SELECT query.

3. In addition to retrieving all data from a column, you can also use the `*` wildcard in a SELECT query to retrieve all columns from a table. For example, if you want to retrieve all the columns for every customer in the `customers` table, the query would be: `SELECT * FROM customers;`. The asterisk `*` tells MySQL to select every column in the table. While this can be useful when you want to view all the data in a table, it's generally better practice to specify only the columns you need, especially when working with large datasets, to improve query performance and readability.

4. When working with SQL, it's common to filter the data you retrieve based on certain conditions. The `WHERE` clause allows you to filter rows by specifying a condition that must be met. For example, if you only want to retrieve customers from a particular city, you can add a `WHERE` clause to your query. Here's an example: `SELECT name FROM customers WHERE city = 'New York';`. This query will return

only the names of customers who live in New York. The `WHERE` clause can be used with a wide variety of conditions, such as matching specific values, comparing numeric values, or checking for null values.

5. SQL allows you to filter data based on multiple conditions by using logical operators like `AND`, `OR`, and `NOT`. For example, if you want to retrieve customers who live in New York or Los Angeles, you can use the OR operator in your query: `SELECT name FROM customers WHERE city = 'New York' OR city = 'Los Angeles';`. Similarly, you can use the `AND` operator to retrieve customers who meet both conditions. For example, to find customers who live in New York and have made a purchase over $100, the query would be: `SELECT name FROM customers WHERE city = 'New York' AND total_purchase > 100;`. These logical operators allow you to combine multiple conditions and filter your data more precisely.

6. In addition to filtering data, the `ORDER BY` clause allows you to sort the results of your query. By default, MySQL sorts data in ascending order (smallest to largest or alphabetical order), but you can specify the sort order by using the `ASC` (ascending) or `DESC` (descending) keywords. For example, if you want to retrieve the customer names in alphabetical order, you can write the query like this: `SELECT name FROM customers ORDER BY name ASC;`. To sort the data in descending order, simply change `ASC` to `DESC`: `SELECT name FROM customers ORDER BY name DESC;`. Sorting data can be very useful when you want to organize the output of your queries.

7. Often, you'll want to retrieve only a subset of the data from your table. For example, you might only want to see the top 10 customers who spent the most money. This can be accomplished using the `LIMIT` clause, which restricts the number of rows returned by the query. Here's an example: `SELECT name, total_purchase FROM customers ORDER BY total_purchase DESC LIMIT 10;`. This query retrieves the names and total purchases of the top 10 customers who spent the most. The `LIMIT` clause is particularly useful when working with large datasets, as it allows you to focus on a specific subset of the data rather than loading everything.

8. Another important SQL concept is the ability to aggregate data using functions like `COUNT()`, `SUM()`, `AVG()`, `MAX()`, and `MIN()`. These aggregate functions allow you to perform calculations on your data, such as counting the number of records or finding the average value of a column. For example, if you want to know how many customers live in each city, you can use the `COUNT()` function: `SELECT city, COUNT(*) FROM customers GROUP BY city;`. This query counts the number of customers in each city and groups the results by city. Aggregating data is especially useful when analyzing large datasets and summarizing key metrics.

9. The `GROUP BY` clause is used in conjunction with aggregate functions to group rows that have the same values in specified columns. This allows you to calculate aggregates on subsets of the data. For example, if you want to find the total amount spent by customers in each city, you could write the following query: `SELECT city, SUM(total_purchase) FROM customers GROUP BY city;`. This query groups the customers by city and then calculates the sum of their purchases in each city. The `GROUP BY` clause is commonly used with aggregate functions to summarize data in meaningful ways.

10. In addition to basic queries, MySQL also supports the `HAVING` clause, which allows you to filter grouped data. Unlike the `WHERE` clause, which filters rows before they are grouped, the `HAVING` clause filters data after it has been grouped. For example, if you want to find cities where the total purchases exceed $10,000, you can use the `HAVING` clause like this: `SELECT city, SUM(total_purchase) FROM customers GROUP BY city HAVING SUM(total_purchase) > 10000;`. The `HAVING` clause is an essential tool for refining the results of grouped data and ensuring that only the data that meets specific criteria is included in the final result.

11. MySQL also allows you to join data from multiple tables, which is an essential feature for working with relational databases. The `JOIN` clause is used to combine rows from two or more tables based on a related column. The most common type of join is the `INNER JOIN`, which returns only the rows where there is a match in both tables. For example, if you have a `customers` table and an `orders` table, and you want to retrieve the names of customers who have placed an order, you can use an `INNER JOIN` like this: `SELECT customers.name FROM customers INNER JOIN orders ON customers.id = orders.customer_id;`. This query retrieves customer names from the `customers` table, but only for those customers who have placed an order in the `orders` table.

12. In addition to the `INNER JOIN`, MySQL supports several other types of joins, including `LEFT JOIN`, `RIGHT JOIN`, and `FULL OUTER JOIN`. A `LEFT JOIN` returns all the rows from the left table (the first table in the query) and the matching rows from the right table. If there is no match, the result will include `NULL` values for columns from the right table. Similarly, a `RIGHT JOIN` returns all the rows from the right table and the matching rows from the left table. The `FULL OUTER JOIN` returns all rows from both tables, with `NULL` values where there is no match. Understanding how to use these different types of joins is crucial for working with relational data in MySQL.

13. Another useful feature of SQL is the ability to use subqueries, which are queries nested within other queries. Subqueries allow you to perform more complex operations, such as filtering data based on the result of another query. For example, if you want to find

customers who have placed orders greater than $100, you could write a query like this: `SELECT name FROM customers WHERE id IN (SELECT customer_id FROM orders WHERE total_purchase > 100);`. This query uses a subquery to retrieve the IDs of customers who have made large orders and then uses those IDs to find the customer names. Subqueries are powerful tools for creating more advanced and dynamic queries.

14. To make your queries more efficient, you can use indexes to speed up data retrieval. An index is a data structure that helps MySQL find rows more quickly, similar to the index in a book that allows you to find a specific topic quickly. You can create an index on one or more columns of a table to speed up searches and queries. For example, if you frequently query customers by their last name, you can create an index on the `last_name` column to improve performance: `CREATE INDEX idx_last_name ON customers(last_name);`. Indexes can significantly improve query performance, especially on large datasets, but they do require additional storage space and can slow down insertions and updates, so it's important to use them wisely.

15. As you continue working with MySQL, you'll encounter more advanced concepts like transactions, normalization, and optimization. These topics will help you improve the design and performance of your databases. In this chapter, however, you've learned the basic building blocks of working with MySQL: how to retrieve, filter, sort, and aggregate data, how to join tables, and how to write subqueries. By mastering these fundamental techniques, you'll be well-equipped to handle more complex database tasks as you continue your journey with MySQL. Keep practicing these commands and concepts, and you'll be ready to take on more advanced topics in the chapters to come.

16. Before moving on to more advanced concepts, it's important to practice writing basic SQL queries regularly. By experimenting with different variations of the `SELECT`, `WHERE`, `ORDER BY`, `GROUP BY`, and `JOIN` clauses, you'll gain confidence in your ability to interact with MySQL. Try using different types of filters, sorting options, and aggregates to see how they affect the results. The more you practice, the more intuitive SQL will become, and you'll be able to handle increasingly complex queries with ease. Remember that practice makes perfect, so take your time with these basic queries and experiment with the different tools that MySQL provides.

17. In this chapter, you've learned the basic building blocks of SQL queries, and you've started to interact with MySQL in a meaningful way. From simple SELECT queries to filtering and sorting data, you now have the tools needed to retrieve and analyze data from MySQL databases. In the next chapter, we'll build on this foundation and explore how to manage databases and tables more effectively, as well as how to modify data using INSERT, UPDATE, and DELETE commands. As you continue learning, remember that SQL is a powerful tool, and the more you practice and experiment, the better you'll become at working with MySQL.

18. Now that you understand the basics of SQL queries, it's important to understand how SQL commands interact with MySQL's underlying data structure. MySQL's ability to

manage large datasets and perform complex operations is rooted in its optimization techniques, which allow it to process queries efficiently. Understanding how MySQL handles indexing, joins, and query execution will give you insight into how to write more efficient and effective queries. In future chapters, we'll delve into performance tuning and optimization strategies, ensuring that your MySQL queries remain fast and scalable.

19. As you continue your journey with MySQL, always keep in mind that database management is both a science and an art. While it's important to understand the theoretical concepts behind relational databases and SQL, the practical skills you develop through hands-on experience will be the most valuable. Keep experimenting with queries, troubleshooting issues, and optimizing your databases. The more real-world experience you gain, the more you'll understand how to apply MySQL's power to solve complex data management problems.

20. To wrap up, you've completed your first set of SQL queries in MySQL. By now, you should feel comfortable writing basic SELECT queries, using WHERE clauses for filtering, sorting and grouping your results, and joining multiple tables. With these foundational skills, you're well-equipped to dive deeper into more advanced topics, such as transactions, data normalization, and database optimization. Keep building on these skills, and as you move forward, you'll unlock the full power of MySQL to manage data in any environment.

Chapter 4: Understanding MySQL Data Types

1. One of the first steps in creating a database is understanding how data is stored in MySQL. Just like in any other relational database system, MySQL uses data types to specify the type of data that a column in a table can hold. These data types are important because they dictate how data is stored, retrieved, and manipulated within the database. Understanding MySQL data types is essential for ensuring that your data is organized efficiently and that queries run smoothly. In this chapter, we'll explore the most common MySQL data types, including numeric types, string types, and date/time types, along with some other specialized types. By the end of this chapter, you'll have a solid understanding of how to choose the right data types for your tables and columns.

2. MySQL has several categories of data types, including numeric, string, date/time, and other specialized types. Numeric data types are used to store numbers, whether integers or decimals. String data types are used to store text or character-based data, such as names, addresses, and descriptions. Date/time data types are used to store temporal information, such as birthdates, timestamps, and durations. Understanding the differences between these types will help you make informed decisions about how to structure your database. Choosing the right data type not only affects the accuracy of your data but also the performance of your queries. For example, using the correct numeric data type can save space and improve query performance, while choosing the wrong one might lead to unnecessary storage overhead or data truncation.

3. The most basic numeric data types in MySQL are integers. MySQL supports several integer types, including `TINYINT`, `SMALLINT`, `MEDIUMINT`, `INT`, and `BIGINT`.

These types are used to store whole numbers, with different sizes depending on how large the number can be. The `TINYINT` type can store values from -128 to 127, while `SMALLINT` can store values from -32,768 to 32,767. The `INT` type is the most commonly used integer type and can store values from -2,147,483,648 to 2,147,483,647. If you need to store larger numbers, `BIGINT` can handle values up to 9 quintillion. Choosing the correct integer type depends on the range of values you expect to store. For example, if you're tracking ages, a `TINYINT` or `SMALLINT` might be sufficient, while if you're storing large user IDs or transaction amounts, an `INT` or `BIGINT` may be necessary.

4. In addition to integer types, MySQL also provides data types for storing decimal numbers. The `DECIMAL` and `NUMERIC` types are used for exact numeric values with a fixed number of decimal places. These types are often used for storing financial data, such as prices or amounts, where precision is crucial. The `DECIMAL` type allows you to specify both the total number of digits and the number of digits after the decimal point. For example, `DECIMAL(10, 2)` would store numbers with up to 10 digits, including two digits after the decimal point. This ensures that financial calculations are accurate and don't suffer from rounding errors that can occur with floating-point types. The `FLOAT` and `DOUBLE` types, on the other hand, are used for storing approximate numeric values with floating decimal points, which are less precise than `DECIMAL`.

5. When choosing a data type for storing numeric values, it's important to consider both the range of values you need to store and the level of precision required. For example, if you're storing prices and need exact precision, `DECIMAL` is the better choice. However, if you're dealing with measurements or scientific data where small rounding errors are acceptable, `FLOAT` or `DOUBLE` might be more appropriate. Always be mindful of the performance implications of your choice. Decimal types tend to use more storage space than integer types, and floating-point numbers may introduce small rounding errors, so it's essential to make the right choice for your use case.

6. String data types in MySQL are used to store text and character-based data. The most common string types are `CHAR`, `VARCHAR`, `TEXT`, and `BLOB`. The `CHAR` data type is used to store fixed-length strings, meaning that the field will always take up the same amount of space, regardless of the length of the string. For example, if you define a `CHAR(10)` column, it will always use 10 bytes of storage, even if the string is shorter than 10 characters. This can be useful for storing data that always has a fixed length, such as country codes or ZIP codes. However, for variable-length strings, the `VARCHAR` data type is more appropriate, as it only uses the space required to store the string, plus a small overhead for the length of the string.

7. The `VARCHAR` type is more flexible than `CHAR` and is widely used for storing variable-length strings, such as names, email addresses, or descriptions. Unlike `CHAR`, `VARCHAR` only uses as much storage as needed, making it more efficient for storing shorter strings. However, `VARCHAR` has a maximum length limit, which can vary depending on the

version of MySQL and the character set used. For example, in MySQL 5.0 and later, `VARCHAR` columns can store up to 65,535 characters, but keep in mind that using very large `VARCHAR` columns may impact performance. If you need to store very large text data, MySQL provides the `TEXT` data type, which can store up to 65,535 characters.

8. MySQL also provides the `TEXT` data type for storing larger amounts of text, such as articles, blog posts, or product descriptions. The `TEXT` type can hold a large number of characters, but it has some limitations compared to `VARCHAR`. For example, `TEXT` columns cannot have an index directly created on them unless they are part of a full-text index. Additionally, `TEXT` values are stored outside the table itself, with only a pointer to the actual data being stored in the table. This can make reading and writing large `TEXT` columns a bit slower than `VARCHAR` columns, which are stored directly in the table.

9. MySQL also provides the `BLOB` (Binary Large Object) data type for storing binary data, such as images, files, or other non-textual data. The `BLOB` type is similar to `TEXT`, but it is used specifically for binary data. Just like `TEXT`, the `BLOB` type can store large amounts of data, up to 65,535 bytes. There are several variations of `BLOB`, including `TINYBLOB`, `BLOB`, `MEDIUMBLOB`, and `LONGBLOB`, which differ in the amount of data they can store. For example, `TINYBLOB` can store up to 255 bytes, while `LONGBLOB` can store up to 4GB of data. When choosing a `BLOB` type, consider the size of the data you plan to store, as well as the performance implications of storing large binary data.

10. MySQL also provides data types for working with date and time values. The most common date and time types are `DATE`, `DATETIME`, `TIMESTAMP`, `TIME`, and `YEAR`. The `DATE` type stores dates in the format `YYYY-MM-DD`, and it is used for storing calendar dates. For example, if you want to store a person's birthdate, you would use the `DATE` type. The `DATETIME` type stores both the date and time, in the format `YYYY-MM-DD HH:MM:SS`. This is useful for storing events that occur at specific times, such as a meeting or a transaction. The `TIMESTAMP` type is similar to `DATETIME`, but it has the added feature of being automatically updated whenever a row is modified. This makes `TIMESTAMP` ideal for tracking when records were created or last updated.

11. The `TIME` type is used for storing time values without a date, such as the duration of an event or the time of day. For example, you might use `TIME` to store the length of a call or the time a bus arrives at a stop. The `YEAR` type is used to store a four-digit year, which can be useful for storing birth years or other year-based information. Understanding how to use these date and time types correctly is crucial for applications that require accurate temporal data.

12. MySQL also supports a variety of specialized data types. One of these is the `BOOLEAN` type, which is used to store logical values, such as `TRUE` or `FALSE`. In MySQL,

BOOLEAN is just a synonym for the `TINYINT(1)` type, where 0 represents `FALSE` and 1 represents `TRUE`. If you need to store logical values in your database, BOOLEAN is a good choice. Another specialized data type is ENUM, which allows you to store one value from a predefined list of values. For example, you could use ENUM to store a list of statuses, such as "active," "inactive," or "pending." The SET data type is similar to ENUM, but it allows you to store multiple values from the predefined list, making it useful for cases where an entity can have more than one status.

13. When designing your database schema, it's important to carefully choose the right data type for each column. Using the correct data type ensures that your data is stored efficiently and accurately. It also helps to maintain data integrity, as the database will enforce rules based on the data type. For example, if you define a column as `DATE`, MySQL will only allow valid date values to be inserted into that column. Similarly, if you define a column as `INT`, MySQL will reject any non-integer values. By understanding the various data types and their purposes, you can design a more effective and reliable database.

14. Another important consideration is the storage space required by each data type. Different data types use different amounts of storage, and it's important to choose the most appropriate type for your data to minimize waste. For example, using `VARCHAR(255)` when you only need 50 characters can lead to unnecessary storage usage. Similarly, choosing a `BIGINT` type for a field that only needs to store small integer values will consume more storage than necessary. As you design your database schema, keep in mind the trade-offs between performance, storage space, and data integrity.

15. As you continue to build and manage MySQL databases, understanding data types will help you create more efficient and optimized structures. By choosing the correct types for your columns, you ensure that your data is stored and processed in the most effective way possible. In this chapter, you've learned about the most common MySQL data types, including numeric, string, date/time, and specialized types. By understanding how to use these types correctly, you're well on your way to mastering MySQL and designing databases that are both functional and performant. In the next chapter, we'll dive deeper into creating and managing MySQL databases and tables, so you can start putting these concepts into practice.

16. Now that you have a better understanding of MySQL's data types, it's important to experiment with them in your own databases. Practice defining tables with various data types, and try inserting, updating, and querying data based on different types. This hands-on experience will solidify your understanding of how data types affect the storage and retrieval of information in MySQL. The more you experiment, the more comfortable you'll become with choosing the right data types for your tables and optimizing your database structure for performance and accuracy.

17. Keep in mind that the choice of data type can impact more than just storage; it also affects how queries are executed. For example, using the appropriate numeric type can

improve the speed of calculations and queries, while using the correct string type can help reduce the overhead when working with text data. As you progress in your MySQL journey, you'll start to see how these choices affect your database's performance and functionality.

18. MySQL data types are a crucial part of designing efficient, effective databases. By selecting the right types for your columns and understanding how they work, you can ensure that your data is stored and processed efficiently. With a solid understanding of MySQL's data types, you are now ready to move forward in your journey, tackling more advanced topics like indexing, optimization, and query performance. Keep practicing with these data types, and soon you'll be able to design complex and powerful databases with ease.

19. As you continue to explore MySQL, always keep in mind that data types are the foundation upon which your database is built. Each decision you make about the type of data to store in a column will have implications for performance, storage, and functionality. By carefully considering the types that best suit your data, you can ensure that your database will perform efficiently and be easy to maintain in the long run. Take time to review the data types available in MySQL and experiment with different configurations to see how they can work together to solve real-world problems.

20. In conclusion, understanding MySQL data types is fundamental to building effective databases. In this chapter, you've learned about numeric types, string types, date/time types, and specialized types, as well as how to choose the best one for each column in your tables. With this knowledge, you're equipped to make informed decisions when creating tables and inserting data. In the next chapter, we'll dive deeper into creating and managing MySQL databases and tables, taking your skills to the next level. Keep practicing with what you've learned so far, and you'll soon be an expert at handling MySQL data types!

Chapter 5: Writing Your First SQL Commands

1. In this chapter, we will begin writing and executing your first SQL commands. While we've covered the basics of data types and structure, the real power of MySQL lies in being able to manipulate your data. SQL (Structured Query Language) allows you to interact with your databases by writing commands that can retrieve, update, and manage data. If you have set up MySQL on your system and created your first database, now is the time to start putting those concepts into action. We will cover the most basic SQL commands, such as `SELECT`, `INSERT`, `UPDATE`, and `DELETE`, which are the foundation of interacting with your data in MySQL. By the end of this chapter, you will be able to write your first SQL commands and execute them within MySQL.

2. The first SQL command you'll learn is the `SELECT` statement, which is used to retrieve data from a table. The syntax for a basic `SELECT` query is quite simple: `SELECT column1, column2 FROM table_name;`. For example, if you have a `customers` table and want to retrieve the customer names, the query would look like

this: `SELECT name FROM customers;`. If you want to retrieve data from multiple columns, simply list the column names separated by commas, like this: `SELECT name, email FROM customers;`. In most cases, you'll want to use `SELECT *` to select all columns in a table, like so: `SELECT * FROM customers;`. This retrieves all the columns from the `customers` table. While `SELECT *` is useful for quick exploration, it's often better to specify only the columns you need to optimize performance.

3. Next, we'll learn how to filter data with the `WHERE` clause, which is one of the most important parts of SQL. The `WHERE` clause allows you to specify conditions that must be met for the data to be included in the results. For example, if you want to retrieve customers who live in New York, the query would be: `SELECT name FROM customers WHERE city = 'New York';`. This query filters the rows, returning only customers whose `city` is "New York." The `WHERE` clause can also handle more complex conditions, such as checking for ranges of values or using logical operators like `AND`, `OR`, and `NOT`. For example, if you want to retrieve customers from New York who have made purchases over $100, you can write the query like this: `SELECT name FROM customers WHERE city = 'New York' AND total_purchase > 100;`.

4. Sometimes, you might want to sort the results of your query. SQL provides the `ORDER BY` clause for this purpose. The `ORDER BY` clause allows you to arrange the results in either ascending or descending order. By default, `ORDER BY` sorts in ascending order, but you can specify the `ASC` keyword to make this explicit. For example, if you want to sort customer names alphabetically, the query would be: `SELECT name FROM customers ORDER BY name;`. If you want the names sorted in reverse (descending) order, you would add the `DESC` keyword: `SELECT name FROM customers ORDER BY name DESC;`. You can also sort by multiple columns by adding more columns to the `ORDER BY` clause, separated by commas, such as `SELECT name, city FROM customers ORDER BY city ASC, name DESC;`.

5. In addition to retrieving specific rows, you might want to limit the number of rows returned by your query. This can be especially useful when working with large datasets. The `LIMIT` clause restricts the number of rows returned. For example, if you want to retrieve only the top 5 customers who made the highest purchases, you can write the query like this: `SELECT name, total_purchase FROM customers ORDER BY total_purchase DESC LIMIT 5;`. This query will return the names and total purchases of the top 5 customers, sorted by the highest total purchase. The `LIMIT` clause is a powerful tool for managing large datasets and ensuring your queries remain fast and efficient.

6. Another powerful feature of SQL is the ability to perform calculations directly within your query. You can use arithmetic operators like `+`, `-`, `*`, and `/` to perform calculations on numeric columns. For example, if you want to calculate the total purchase amount for each customer including tax, you could write a query like this: `SELECT name, total_purchase, total_purchase * 1.1 AS total_with_tax FROM customers;`. In this query, the `* 1.1` operation multiplies each customer's purchase by 1.1 to add a 10% tax. The `AS` keyword allows you to assign an alias to the calculated column, so in this case, the new column will be named `total_with_tax`. Using calculations in your queries can help you quickly perform analysis without needing to modify the underlying data.

7. So far, we've only covered retrieving data, but SQL also allows you to modify the data in your database. One of the most common ways to modify data is by using the `INSERT INTO` statement. This command is used to add new rows to a table. The syntax for `INSERT INTO` is: `INSERT INTO table_name (column1, column2, ...) VALUES (value1, value2, ...);`. For example, to insert a new customer into the `customers` table, you might write: `INSERT INTO customers (name, email, city, total_purchase) VALUES ('John Doe', 'john.doe@example.com', 'New York', 150);`. This query inserts a new customer with the specified values into the corresponding columns of the `customers` table. Always make sure to provide values in the correct order corresponding to the column names.

8. SQL also allows you to modify existing data using the `UPDATE` statement. The `UPDATE` command is used when you need to change the values in one or more columns for specific rows. For example, if a customer's email address changes, you can update their record with the following query: `UPDATE customers SET email = 'new.email@example.com' WHERE name = 'John Doe';`. This query updates the `email` column for the customer whose name is "John Doe." The `WHERE` clause is critical in the `UPDATE` statement because without it, all rows in the table would be updated. Always double-check your `WHERE` clause when using `UPDATE`, as an incorrect clause can result in modifying unintended rows.

9. Just as you can update data, you can also delete data using the `DELETE` statement. The `DELETE` statement removes rows from a table based on the condition you provide. For example, if you need to delete a customer who no longer exists in the system, you could write: `DELETE FROM customers WHERE name = 'John Doe';`. This query removes the row where the name is "John Doe." It's important to be cautious when using `DELETE` statements, especially without a `WHERE` clause. If you omit the `WHERE` clause, all rows in the table will be deleted, which can be catastrophic for your data. Always make sure you have the correct conditions before running a `DELETE` query.

10. A very useful feature in MySQL is the ability to combine multiple SQL commands into one query. For example, you can perform an `INSERT` to add new data, then use `UPDATE` to change specific data, and finish with a `SELECT` to verify the changes. By combining commands, you can automate tasks and perform multiple operations in a single transaction. Here's an example of a sequence of commands: `INSERT INTO customers (name, email) VALUES ('Jane Doe', 'jane.doe@example.com'); UPDATE customers SET email = 'jane.newemail@example.com' WHERE name = 'Jane Doe'; SELECT * FROM customers WHERE name = 'Jane Doe';`. This sequence adds a new customer, updates their email address, and then retrieves the updated information in one go.

11. Sometimes, you may want to delete all rows in a table but keep the structure of the table intact. This can be achieved using the `TRUNCATE TABLE` command. Unlike `DELETE`, which removes rows one by one, `TRUNCATE TABLE` quickly removes all rows in a table, without logging individual row deletions. The syntax for truncating a table is as follows: `TRUNCATE TABLE table_name;`. For example, if you want to clear all the data in the `customers` table but leave the table structure and columns intact, you would write: `TRUNCATE TABLE customers;`. This operation is much faster than `DELETE` because it doesn't log individual row deletions and doesn't fire triggers, but it's important to note that it cannot be rolled back in most cases.

12. Another feature of SQL is the ability to manage the structure of your tables using `ALTER TABLE`. This command allows you to make changes to the table's columns, such as adding new columns, renaming columns, or changing the data type of a column. For example, if you want to add a new column to the `customers` table for storing the customer's phone number, you would write: `ALTER TABLE customers ADD COLUMN phone_number VARCHAR(15);`. This adds a new column called `phone_number` with the `VARCHAR(15)` data type to the table. You can also modify columns or drop them using `ALTER TABLE`, making it a flexible tool for managing your table structure.

13. While it's important to know how to write basic SQL commands, it's equally important to understand the concept of transactions. A transaction in MySQL allows you to execute multiple queries as a single unit of work. This is useful for ensuring that changes to the database are only committed if all parts of the transaction are successful. For example, if you're transferring money between two accounts, you would want to ensure that both the debit and credit operations are successful before committing the transaction. The basic syntax for transactions is: `START TRANSACTION;`, followed by your SQL commands, and then either `COMMIT;` to apply the changes or `ROLLBACK;` to undo them. Transactions are crucial for maintaining data integrity and consistency, especially in multi-step operations.

14. In addition to basic SQL commands, MySQL also supports advanced functionality, such as creating and managing indexes, writing stored procedures, and working with views. These features help you manage larger databases more efficiently and automate common tasks. However, as a beginner, it's important to master the basic SQL commands first, as they form the foundation for more advanced operations. As you continue your journey with MySQL, you'll have opportunities to explore these advanced topics in greater detail.

15. In this chapter, you've written your first SQL commands to interact with your MySQL database. You've learned how to retrieve data with `SELECT`, filter results with `WHERE`, sort and limit results with `ORDER BY` and `LIMIT`, and modify data with `INSERT`, `UPDATE`, and `DELETE`. These fundamental commands are essential for working with MySQL, and you'll use them regularly as you build more complex queries and applications. The next chapter will dive deeper into creating and managing MySQL databases and tables, exploring how to structure your data efficiently and optimize performance. By continuing to practice these SQL commands and incorporating them into your workflow, you'll become proficient in MySQL and ready to tackle more advanced topics.

Chapter 5: Writing Your First SQL Commands (continued)

16. Now that you have learned the basics of SQL commands, it's important to continue practicing. SQL is a language that you get better at the more you use it. One of the best ways to become proficient is by writing queries on your own, experimenting with different combinations of clauses, operators, and commands. Start by creating small tables with different data types and practice retrieving and manipulating data in various ways. Use the `SELECT` statement to explore different filters and sorting options. Write `UPDATE` commands to change data in specific rows and try different conditions with the `WHERE` clause. Try `INSERT` statements to add new rows and `DELETE` statements to remove data. Each time you write and execute a query, try to think about how the query works and how the data is affected.

17. As you get more comfortable with basic SQL commands, consider the performance of your queries. For example, if you're working with a large dataset, queries that use `SELECT *` or lack proper indexing can slow down your system. It's important to optimize your queries for better performance. One way to do this is by selecting only the columns you need with `SELECT`, rather than using `SELECT *`, which returns all columns. In addition, using `WHERE` clauses that filter on indexed columns will often improve query performance. For example, if you have an `index` on a `customer_id` column, using `WHERE customer_id = 101` will be much faster than querying columns that are not indexed. Understanding and optimizing queries for performance is a critical skill that you'll develop over time.

18. Beyond just retrieving and modifying data, SQL also allows you to control how data is represented in your database. You can use constraints, like `NOT NULL`, `DEFAULT`, and `UNIQUE`, to ensure that your data meets specific conditions. For example, if you want to

make sure every customer has an email address, you could define the `email` column with the `NOT NULL` constraint to ensure that no null values are allowed. Similarly, you could set a `DEFAULT` value for a column, such as setting a default value for the `status` column of a new customer to be "active". The `UNIQUE` constraint ensures that no two rows in a column have the same value, which is useful for columns like email addresses or usernames. These constraints help ensure data integrity, prevent errors, and provide structure to your tables.

19. SQL also supports the use of aliases to make your queries more readable. An alias is a temporary name you give to a table or a column in a query, making the result set easier to understand. For example, when performing complex queries, you may want to give a column a more user-friendly name: `SELECT name AS customer_name FROM customers;`. Here, the `AS customer_name` part renames the `name` column to `customer_name` in the result set. Similarly, table aliases are useful when you're working with multiple tables and want to keep your query clear. For example, if you are joining two tables, you can give each table an alias for brevity: `SELECT c.name, o.order_date FROM customers AS c INNER JOIN orders AS o ON c.id = o.customer_id;`. Using aliases helps make your SQL queries more readable, especially when they involve multiple tables and complex conditions.

20. In addition to writing queries, it's important to understand how to debug and troubleshoot SQL commands. When running a query, MySQL may return errors if something is wrong with your syntax or logic. Common errors include missing commas between columns, incorrect column names, or improper use of operators in a `WHERE` clause. For example, if you accidentally write `WHERE total_purchase == 100` instead of `WHERE total_purchase = 100`, MySQL will return an error because the == operator is not recognized in SQL. Learning how to read and interpret error messages is an essential part of writing efficient SQL queries. Most of the time, MySQL will provide hints or error codes that can help you identify and fix issues. Don't be afraid to review your query carefully, consult MySQL's documentation, or search online for solutions when you encounter an error.

21. Another important aspect of SQL is understanding how to work with aggregate functions, such as `COUNT()`, `SUM()`, `AVG()`, `MIN()`, and `MAX()`. These functions are useful for performing calculations and summarizing data within a query. For example, if you want to find the total number of customers, you could write the query: `SELECT COUNT(*) FROM customers;`. Similarly, to find the highest total purchase among customers, you could use the `MAX()` function: `SELECT MAX(total_purchase) FROM customers;`. Aggregate functions can also be used with the `GROUP BY` clause to group results by specific criteria. For example, if you want to find the total purchase amount for each city, you could use the following query: `SELECT city, SUM(total_purchase) FROM customers`

`GROUP BY city;`. Aggregates are a powerful way to analyze and summarize data in MySQL.

22. One of the features that makes SQL especially powerful is its ability to work with multiple tables. Often, you'll need to retrieve data from more than one table, and SQL's `JOIN` clause allows you to do just that. The most common type of join is the `INNER JOIN`, which retrieves records that have matching values in both tables. For example, if you have a `customers` table and an `orders` table, and you want to retrieve customer names and their order totals, you could use a query like this: `SELECT customers.name, orders.total_amount FROM customers INNER JOIN orders ON customers.id = orders.customer_id;`. This query returns only the customers who have placed orders. There are other types of joins, such as `LEFT JOIN` and `RIGHT JOIN`, that allow you to include records from one table even when no matching rows exist in the other table.

23. Sometimes, you'll need to run subqueries, which are queries within a query. Subqueries allow you to perform more complex operations and retrieve results that depend on the outcome of another query. For example, to find customers who made a purchase of more than $100, you can use a subquery like this: `SELECT name FROM customers WHERE id IN (SELECT customer_id FROM orders WHERE total_amount > 100);`. The subquery inside the parentheses returns the list of customer IDs with orders greater than $100, and the main query uses that list to fetch the customer names. Subqueries are powerful tools for handling more complex conditions that cannot be easily expressed with simple filters.

24. As you write more SQL queries, you will find that your queries become more complex, involving multiple joins, subqueries, and aggregate functions. While this can make your queries more powerful, it can also make them harder to read and maintain. This is where organizing your SQL code becomes important. You should strive to write clear, well-organized queries by using proper indentation and formatting. For example, break up long queries into multiple lines to make each part of the query easy to understand. Always use aliases to simplify the query, and add comments where necessary to explain the purpose of complex sections of the query. Writing clean and organized SQL will help you and others maintain and modify the code in the future.

25. By now, you've learned how to write your first SQL commands and interact with MySQL. You've mastered basic data retrieval with `SELECT`, learned how to filter and sort data with `WHERE` and `ORDER BY`, and understood how to manipulate data with `INSERT`, `UPDATE`, and `DELETE`. You've also been introduced to more advanced concepts, such as joins, subqueries, and aggregate functions. As you continue practicing and working with MySQL, remember that SQL is a powerful tool that can be used to manage, analyze, and manipulate data in various ways. The more you practice writing SQL queries, the more proficient you'll become. In the next chapter, we'll dive deeper

into managing MySQL databases and tables, including how to create and modify them effectively. Keep experimenting with what you've learned so far, and your skills will continue to improve with each query you write.

Chapter 6: Exploring MySQL Databases and Tables

1. In this chapter, we will dive deeper into the essential building blocks of MySQL: databases and tables. A database is where all of your data is stored in MySQL, while tables are the structures within the database that organize the data. As you begin working with MySQL, understanding how to create, manage, and modify databases and tables is crucial. In this chapter, we will cover the steps to create a database, how to create and define tables within that database, and how to perform essential tasks like altering and dropping tables. By the end of this chapter, you will be comfortable managing your MySQL databases and tables, laying the foundation for building complex data structures.

2. To start working with MySQL, you must first create a database. The command to create a database in MySQL is `CREATE DATABASE`. The basic syntax is: `CREATE DATABASE database_name;`. For example, if you want to create a database called `company`, you would execute: `CREATE DATABASE company;`. Once a database is created, you can switch to it using the `USE` statement, which tells MySQL which database to work with. For example, `USE company;` will switch to the `company` database. From here, you can begin creating tables and working with your data. It's important to note that a database in MySQL serves as a container for tables, views, indexes, and other database objects, organizing all your data in a logical manner.

3. After creating a database, the next step is to create tables within that database. Tables are where the actual data is stored. To create a table, you use the `CREATE TABLE` statement, which allows you to define the table structure, including its columns, data types, and constraints. The basic syntax of the `CREATE TABLE` statement is: `CREATE TABLE table_name (column1 datatype, column2 datatype, ...);`. For example, if you want to create a table called `employees` with columns for `id`, `name`, `position`, and `salary`, you could write the following query: `CREATE TABLE employees (id INT PRIMARY KEY, name VARCHAR(100), position VARCHAR(50), salary DECIMAL(10, 2));`. This command creates a table with the specified columns and data types. The `id` column is defined as an integer and serves as the primary key, ensuring that each employee has a unique identifier.

4. Each column in a table must have a data type that specifies the kind of data that can be stored in that column. As we discussed in Chapter 4, MySQL offers a variety of data types, including numeric types, string types, and date/time types. When creating a table, you must choose the appropriate data type for each column based on the data you plan to store. For example, if you have a column for storing employee names, you might choose the `VARCHAR` data type, which is suitable for variable-length text data. If you're storing

salary information, you would use the `DECIMAL` type to ensure accurate financial calculations. Choosing the right data type ensures data integrity and optimizes the performance of your queries.

5. In addition to data types, MySQL allows you to define constraints on columns when creating a table. Constraints ensure that the data entered into a column meets certain conditions. Common constraints include `NOT NULL`, `DEFAULT`, `UNIQUE`, and `CHECK`. For example, if you want to make sure that the `name` column in the `employees` table cannot be empty, you can add a `NOT NULL` constraint: `name VARCHAR(100) NOT NULL`. Similarly, you can set a default value for a column, so that if no value is provided, the column will automatically take that default value. For instance, `position VARCHAR(50) DEFAULT 'Employee'` ensures that if no position is specified, it will default to "Employee."

6. After creating a table, you might want to modify its structure. MySQL provides the `ALTER TABLE` statement for this purpose. The `ALTER TABLE` command allows you to add, modify, or drop columns in an existing table. For example, if you want to add a column for `hire_date` to the `employees` table, you can write the following query: `ALTER TABLE employees ADD hire_date DATE;`. This command adds a new column called `hire_date` with the `DATE` data type. If you want to modify an existing column, such as changing the data type of the `salary` column to allow more decimal places, you could use: `ALTER TABLE employees MODIFY salary DECIMAL(12, 2);`. Additionally, you can drop a column that is no longer needed with the `DROP COLUMN` option, like so: `ALTER TABLE employees DROP COLUMN hire_date;`.

7. Managing primary and foreign keys is another important aspect of working with tables. A primary key uniquely identifies each record in a table and ensures that no two rows can have the same value for that column. When creating a table, you can define a primary key using the `PRIMARY KEY` constraint. For example, in the `employees` table, you might define the `id` column as the primary key: `id INT PRIMARY KEY`. Foreign keys are used to establish relationships between tables by linking a column in one table to the primary key of another table. To create a foreign key, use the `FOREIGN KEY` constraint. For example, if you have a `departments` table and you want to link the `department_id` column in the `employees` table to the `id` column in the `departments` table, you would write: `FOREIGN KEY (department_id) REFERENCES departments(id);`. Foreign keys help maintain referential integrity and prevent invalid data from being entered into the database.

8. Once a table is created, you can insert data into it using the `INSERT INTO` statement. This command allows you to add new rows to a table. The syntax for the `INSERT INTO` statement is: `INSERT INTO table_name (column1, column2, ...) VALUES (value1, value2, ...);`. For example, if

you want to insert a new employee into the `employees` table, you could write: `INSERT INTO employees (id, name, position, salary) VALUES (1, 'John Doe', 'Software Engineer', 75000.00);`. This statement adds a new row to the `employees` table with the specified values. It's important to ensure that the values you insert match the data types and constraints of the columns in the table.

9. Similarly, to retrieve data from a table, you can use the `SELECT` statement, as discussed in Chapter 5. For example, if you want to view all the employees in the `employees` table, you can write: `SELECT * FROM employees;`. This will return all rows and columns from the `employees` table. To retrieve specific columns, you can modify the `SELECT` statement: `SELECT name, position FROM employees;`. You can also use the `WHERE` clause to filter the results based on specific conditions, like: `SELECT * FROM employees WHERE salary > 70000;`. This query will return only employees whose salary is greater than $70,000.

10. MySQL also provides the `DROP TABLE` statement, which allows you to permanently delete a table and all of its data. This command is useful when you want to remove a table that is no longer needed. The syntax for dropping a table is simple: `DROP TABLE table_name;`. For example, if you want to delete the `employees` table, you would write: `DROP TABLE employees;`. Be cautious when using the `DROP TABLE` statement, as this action cannot be undone, and all data in the table will be lost.

11. In addition to managing tables, MySQL offers the ability to create views, which are virtual tables based on the result of a query. A view allows you to store a complex query that you can reuse multiple times, making it easier to work with frequently used data. The syntax for creating a view is: `CREATE VIEW view_name AS SELECT query;`. For example, if you want to create a view that shows the names of employees and their salaries, you could write: `CREATE VIEW employee_salaries AS SELECT name, salary FROM employees;`. You can then query the view just like a regular table: `SELECT * FROM employee_salaries;`. Views can simplify queries, but remember that they do not store data—they are dynamically generated based on the underlying tables.

12. In addition to views, MySQL supports stored procedures, which are a set of SQL commands that can be executed as a single unit. Stored procedures are useful for encapsulating complex logic, reducing code repetition, and improving performance. To create a stored procedure, you use the `CREATE PROCEDURE` statement. For example, you might write: `CREATE PROCEDURE get_employee_salary(IN employee_id INT) BEGIN SELECT salary FROM employees WHERE id = employee_id; END;`. This procedure accepts an input parameter (`employee_id`) and returns the salary of the employee with that ID. Once created, you can execute the stored procedure using the `CALL` statement: `CALL`

`get_employee_salary(1);`. Stored procedures are an essential tool for managing and automating SQL operations.

13. As you continue to build and work with MySQL databases, it's important to keep your tables organized and well-structured. Proper naming conventions for tables and columns, as well as logical data types and constraints, will make your database easier to manage and maintain. In this chapter, you've learned how to create and manage databases, create and modify tables, and interact with data using SQL commands. The skills you've gained will serve as the foundation for designing more complex databases and queries.

14. As you practice creating databases and tables, try experimenting with more advanced features like creating indexes, using full-text searches, and working with transactions. These features will allow you to build more efficient and scalable database applications. By mastering table design and database management, you will be able to handle large datasets and create powerful, dynamic applications.

15. In conclusion, understanding how to create, manage, and modify databases and tables is essential for any MySQL user. With these foundational skills, you are well on your way to becoming proficient in MySQL database management. In the next chapter, we will explore how to manipulate and query data more efficiently using joins, subqueries, and advanced filtering techniques. Keep practicing with the commands and concepts covered in this chapter, and soon you'll be able to build robust and optimized databases.

As you continue to work with MySQL, it's crucial to understand how to manage and optimize your databases and tables effectively. One of the first steps in database management is to ensure that your data remains clean and well-organized. Proper table design, choosing the correct data types, and applying constraints will help ensure data integrity and prevent errors down the line. As you build more complex databases, you will likely have to manage multiple tables, each containing different types of data. Knowing how to structure your tables in a way that minimizes redundancy and ensures efficient access is critical to maintaining a scalable database.

A common practice in database design is normalization, which is the process of organizing data to reduce redundancy and improve data integrity. Normalization involves breaking down large, complex tables into smaller, more manageable tables and establishing relationships between them. For example, instead of storing employee and department information in the same table, you might create two separate tables—one for `employees` and one for `departments`—and link them with a foreign key relationship. By doing this, you minimize redundant data, which can reduce storage requirements and simplify data management. Understanding the principles of normalization, such as first normal form (1NF), second normal form (2NF), and third normal form (3NF), will help you create more efficient and effective database structures.

Indexing is another important concept when working with MySQL tables. An index is a data structure that helps MySQL quickly locate rows in a table without having to scan the entire table. Indexes can significantly speed up query performance, especially when working with large datasets. You can create indexes on columns that are frequently queried, such as primary keys, foreign keys, or columns involved in filtering. The syntax for creating an index is as follows:

`CREATE INDEX index_name ON table_name (column_name);`. For example, if you frequently query customers by their `email`, you might create an index on the `email` column like this: `CREATE INDEX idx_email ON customers (email);`. While indexes improve read performance, it's important to note that they can slow down write operations, such as `INSERT`, `UPDATE`, and `DELETE`, since the index needs to be updated whenever data is modified.

Another advanced technique for optimizing table performance is partitioning. Partitioning involves splitting a large table into smaller, more manageable pieces, called partitions, based on certain criteria. Partitioning can improve query performance and simplify database management, especially when dealing with huge amounts of data. MySQL supports several types of partitioning, including range partitioning, list partitioning, and hash partitioning. For example, if you have a `sales` table that contains data for several years, you could partition the table by year, allowing queries that target specific years to perform much faster. The syntax for partitioning a table involves adding the `PARTITION BY` clause when creating the table: `CREATE TABLE sales (id INT, amount DECIMAL(10,2), sale_date DATE) PARTITION BY RANGE (YEAR(sale_date)) (PARTITION p0 VALUES LESS THAN (2010), PARTITION p1 VALUES LESS THAN (2015), PARTITION p2 VALUES LESS THAN (2020));`. Partitioning is particularly useful when working with very large datasets, but it requires careful planning and management.

In addition to managing data and optimizing performance, you'll also need to keep your tables secure. MySQL offers a variety of options for securing access to your tables, ensuring that only authorized users can modify or view the data. You can control access using MySQL's user management and permissions system. The `GRANT` command allows you to specify what actions a user can perform on specific databases or tables. For example, if you want to grant a user permission to read from the `employees` table but not modify it, you could use: `GRANT SELECT ON company.employees TO 'username'@'host';`. You can also grant more specific privileges, such as `INSERT`, `UPDATE`, or `DELETE`, depending on the level of access required. Regularly reviewing and auditing user privileges is essential for ensuring that your data remains secure, especially when working in multi-user environments.

In some cases, you may need to back up your MySQL databases and tables to protect against data loss. MySQL provides several methods for backing up data, including using the `mysqldump` command-line tool or using MySQL Workbench for a graphical interface. `mysqldump` allows you to create a backup of your database by exporting the data and structure into a file, which can later be restored if needed. The basic syntax for using `mysqldump` is: `mysqldump -u username -p database_name > backup_file.sql;`. This will create a backup of the `database_name` and save it to a file called `backup_file.sql`. It's important to regularly back up your databases to prevent data loss caused by hardware failures, accidental deletions, or other issues. You can also automate backups by scheduling regular backups using cron jobs (on Linux) or Task Scheduler (on Windows).

Restoring a MySQL database from a backup is just as important as creating backups in the first place. In the event of data loss or corruption, you can use the `mysql` command-line tool to restore your database from a backup file. To restore a database from a backup, you would use the following syntax: `mysql -u username -p database_name < backup_file.sql;`. This command imports the data from the `backup_file.sql` file back into the specified database. It's crucial to regularly test your backup and restore processes to ensure they work as expected and that you can recover your data when needed.

As you continue to work with MySQL databases and tables, you'll also need to monitor the health and performance of your system. MySQL provides several tools for monitoring server status and optimizing queries, such as the `SHOW STATUS` and `EXPLAIN` commands. The `SHOW STATUS` command provides information about the current state of the MySQL server, including details about connections, queries, and memory usage. The `EXPLAIN` command is used to analyze the execution plan of a query, helping you understand how MySQL retrieves data and identifying potential bottlenecks. By regularly monitoring your database's performance, you can proactively identify and resolve issues before they affect your application.

Understanding how to work with MySQL databases and tables is a fundamental skill for anyone using MySQL to manage data. In this chapter, you've learned how to create and manage databases and tables, alter table structures, create indexes, partition tables, and manage user access. You've also explored important topics such as backing up and restoring data, securing your database, and optimizing performance. Mastering these essential skills will enable you to create well-organized, efficient, and secure MySQL databases that can handle a wide range of applications.

As you continue working with MySQL, keep practicing the techniques you've learned in this chapter. Experiment with creating different types of tables, adding indexes, and managing database access. The more you work with MySQL, the more comfortable you will become with the tools and techniques available for managing databases and tables. In the next chapter, we will dive into more advanced querying techniques, such as joins, subqueries, and complex filtering, which will allow you to extract and manipulate data more effectively. By continuing to build your skills, you'll be able to tackle increasingly complex database challenges and become proficient in MySQL database management.

Chapter 7: Filtering and Sorting Data in MySQL

1. In this chapter, we will explore how to filter and sort data in MySQL, two of the most fundamental operations when working with databases. Whether you are retrieving a small set of data or working with large datasets, filtering and sorting are essential for narrowing down the results and organizing them in a meaningful way. The `WHERE` clause is used for filtering data, and the `ORDER BY` clause is used for sorting the results of a query. Understanding how to effectively use these clauses will allow you to write more powerful and efficient SQL queries. By the end of this chapter, you will be able to filter data based on specific conditions and sort your results in ascending or descending order.

2. Filtering data in MySQL is done with the WHERE clause. The WHERE clause allows you to specify conditions that must be met for a row to be included in the result set. The basic syntax for a query with a WHERE clause is: `SELECT column1, column2 FROM table_name WHERE condition;`. For example, if you want to retrieve all customers from the `customers` table who live in "New York", the query would be: `SELECT * FROM customers WHERE city = 'New York';`. The WHERE clause can be used with any column to filter the data based on specific values, whether those values are text, numbers, or dates. It's a powerful tool for narrowing down your results and getting only the data you need.

3. The WHERE clause can also be used with comparison operators such as =, !=, <, >, <=, and >= to filter data based on specific conditions. For example, if you want to find customers who have made purchases greater than $100, you could use the > operator in the WHERE clause: `SELECT * FROM customers WHERE total_purchase > 100;`. Similarly, you can use the <= operator to retrieve customers whose purchases are less than or equal to $100: `SELECT * FROM customers WHERE total_purchase <= 100;`. These operators allow you to filter data based on numerical values, dates, and other measurable attributes.

4. In addition to comparison operators, MySQL also supports logical operators that allow you to combine multiple conditions in the WHERE clause. The most common logical operators are AND, OR, and NOT. For example, if you want to retrieve customers who live in "New York" and have made purchases greater than $100, you can combine two conditions using the AND operator: `SELECT * FROM customers WHERE city = 'New York' AND total_purchase > 100;`. Alternatively, you can use the OR operator to retrieve customers who live in either "New York" or "Los Angeles": `SELECT * FROM customers WHERE city = 'New York' OR city = 'Los Angeles';`. The NOT operator is used to exclude data that matches a certain condition. For example, to retrieve customers who are not from "New York", you would write: `SELECT * FROM customers WHERE NOT city = 'New York';`.

5. You can also filter data based on patterns using the LIKE operator. The LIKE operator is used to search for a specified pattern in a column. For example, if you want to find all customers whose name starts with "J", you can use the LIKE operator with the % wildcard: `SELECT * FROM customers WHERE name LIKE 'J%';`. The % wildcard matches any sequence of characters, while the _ wildcard matches a single character. For instance, `LIKE 'J__n'` would match "John" and "Jane" but not "Jack". The LIKE operator is useful for performing partial matches, especially with text fields such as names and addresses.

6. The IN operator is another useful way to filter data. It allows you to match a column value against a list of possible values. For example, if you want to retrieve customers who live in either "New York", "Los Angeles", or "Chicago", you can use the IN operator: `SELECT * FROM customers WHERE city IN ('New York', 'Los Angeles', 'Chicago');`. This query returns all customers whose city is in the list of specified cities. The IN operator can also be used with numeric or date values, making it a versatile tool for filtering based on multiple conditions.

7. For working with NULL values, MySQL provides the IS NULL and IS NOT NULL operators. These operators allow you to filter data based on whether a column contains a NULL value. For example, if you want to find customers who do not have an email address, you could write the query: `SELECT * FROM customers WHERE email IS NULL;`. Conversely, if you want to retrieve customers who have provided an email address, you can use IS NOT NULL: `SELECT * FROM customers WHERE email IS NOT NULL;`. Using these operators ensures that you can properly handle and filter missing or undefined values in your data.

8. In addition to basic filtering, MySQL also allows you to filter data based on date and time values. MySQL provides a range of date functions to work with date columns, and you can filter results using specific date ranges. For example, if you want to retrieve all orders placed in the last 30 days, you could write a query like this: `SELECT * FROM orders WHERE order_date >= CURDATE() - INTERVAL 30 DAY;`. The CURDATE() function returns the current date, and the INTERVAL keyword allows you to specify a time interval. You can also filter data based on specific date parts (e.g., year, month, day) using functions like YEAR(), MONTH(), and DAY(). For example, to retrieve orders placed in January 2021, you could write: `SELECT * FROM orders WHERE YEAR(order_date) = 2021 AND MONTH(order_date) = 1;`.

9. Once you've filtered your data, you may want to sort it to make it more readable or to find the highest or lowest values. The ORDER BY clause is used to sort the results of a query. By default, ORDER BY sorts data in ascending order, but you can specify whether you want the data to be sorted in ascending or descending order. The basic syntax for the ORDER BY clause is: `SELECT column1, column2 FROM table_name ORDER BY column1 [ASC|DESC];`. For example, to retrieve customer names sorted by the total purchase in descending order, you would write: `SELECT name, total_purchase FROM customers ORDER BY total_purchase DESC;`. To sort the data in ascending order, you can either omit the ASC keyword or explicitly use ASC: `SELECT name, total_purchase FROM customers ORDER BY total_purchase ASC;`.

10. You can sort data by multiple columns by separating the column names with commas in the ORDER BY clause. For example, if you want to sort customers by their city in

alphabetical order and, within each city, sort them by total purchase in descending order, you could write: `SELECT name, city, total_purchase FROM customers ORDER BY city ASC, total_purchase DESC;`. Sorting by multiple columns is useful when you want to organize your data in a hierarchical way, where the first column represents the primary sorting order and the subsequent columns define secondary sorting criteria.

11. MySQL also allows you to limit the number of rows returned by a query using the `LIMIT` clause, which is particularly useful when you're working with large datasets. The `LIMIT` clause restricts the result set to a specified number of rows. For example, if you only want to retrieve the top 5 customers by total purchase, you can write: `SELECT name, total_purchase FROM customers ORDER BY total_purchase DESC LIMIT 5;`. This query returns the names and purchase totals of the top 5 customers who have spent the most money. You can also use the `LIMIT` clause in conjunction with `OFFSET` to paginate your results, for example, to retrieve the next set of 5 records: `SELECT name, total_purchase FROM customers ORDER BY total_purchase DESC LIMIT 5 OFFSET 5;`.

12. Sorting and filtering data together often allows you to perform more complex operations. For example, if you want to retrieve the top 10 customers from "New York" who have spent more than $100, you can combine both filtering and sorting: `SELECT name, total_purchase FROM customers WHERE city = 'New York' AND total_purchase > 100 ORDER BY total_purchase DESC LIMIT 10;`. This query filters customers from New York who have made purchases over $100, sorts them by the total purchase amount in descending order, and limits the result to the top 10 records. Combining filtering and sorting allows you to narrow down and organize your data in meaningful ways.

13. Another useful feature in MySQL is the ability to filter and sort results based on calculations or aggregated values. As mentioned in previous chapters, MySQL's aggregate functions like `COUNT()`, `SUM()`, `AVG()`, `MIN()`, and `MAX()` can help you perform calculations on your data. After using these functions, you can apply filtering and sorting to the results. For example, if you want to find the total sales for each product and sort them by total sales in descending order, you can write a query like this: `SELECT product_id, SUM(sales_amount) AS total_sales FROM sales GROUP BY product_id ORDER BY total_sales DESC;`. This query groups the data by product ID, calculates the total sales for each product, and sorts the results by the total sales.

14. When working with complex datasets, it is essential to use filtering and sorting effectively to organize and present the data in a way that makes sense. By mastering the use of the `WHERE` and `ORDER BY` clauses, you will be able to write more efficient queries and retrieve the exact data you need. Additionally, combining filtering and sorting

with other advanced features, such as aggregate functions and joins, will allow you to perform more sophisticated analysis on your data.

15. In this chapter, we've covered the basics of filtering and sorting data in MySQL. You've learned how to use the `WHERE` clause to filter data based on specific conditions, how to use comparison, logical, and pattern matching operators, and how to sort your results using the `ORDER BY` clause. You've also explored the use of `LIMIT` for restricting the number of rows returned. By mastering these techniques, you'll be able to write more powerful and efficient queries that help you retrieve and analyze data in meaningful ways. In the next chapter, we will explore how to work with MySQL joins to combine data from multiple tables, which will further enhance your ability to analyze complex datasets.

As you progress in MySQL, another important skill to master is filtering and sorting data based on more complex conditions. Combining different filtering techniques within a single query is an essential way to fine-tune your results. For example, you may want to filter data based on both textual conditions and numerical conditions, or combine multiple logical operators. Let's say you want to find customers who live in either "New York" or "Los Angeles" and whose total purchase exceeds $500. You would use the `OR` operator for the cities and the `AND` operator for the purchase condition: `SELECT * FROM customers WHERE (city = 'New York' OR city = 'Los Angeles') AND total_purchase > 500;`. The use of parentheses here ensures the conditions are grouped correctly and applied in the intended order.

It's also important to consider edge cases when filtering and sorting. For example, dealing with NULL values can sometimes result in unexpected behavior if not handled properly. SQL's `IS NULL` and `IS NOT NULL` operators are essential for filtering data that contains NULLs. Suppose you have a table of customers, some of whom have missing email addresses. If you want to retrieve only customers who have an email address, you would write the query: `SELECT * FROM customers WHERE email IS NOT NULL;`. On the other hand, to retrieve customers who do not have an email address, you would use: `SELECT * FROM customers WHERE email IS NULL;`. It's important to be mindful of how NULL values can affect your filtering logic and ensure they are properly handled.

Another common use case when filtering and sorting data is the need to deal with ranges. MySQL provides several options for working with ranges of values, especially when dealing with numeric or date data. The `BETWEEN` operator is particularly useful when filtering data within a specific range. For example, if you want to retrieve orders placed between January 1st and December 31st of 2021, you would write: `SELECT * FROM orders WHERE order_date BETWEEN '2021-01-01' AND '2021-12-31';`. The `BETWEEN` operator works for both numerical and date data, making it versatile and useful when you need to filter data that falls within a certain range. You can also combine `BETWEEN` with other operators for more complex filtering.

In addition to filtering data, you may also need to sort it in a way that makes it more useful for your analysis. The `ORDER BY` clause is a powerful tool for sorting your results, allowing you to sort the data in either ascending (`ASC`) or descending (`DESC`) order. As discussed, you can sort data by one or more columns. If you want to sort customer names alphabetically and, within each name, sort them by their total purchase in descending order, you can write: `SELECT name, total_purchase FROM customers ORDER BY name ASC, total_purchase DESC;`. Sorting by multiple columns is useful when you need to prioritize one criterion over another, and it gives you flexibility in how the data is presented.

Sorting can also be crucial when you want to work with only a subset of the data, such as retrieving the top or bottom values in a table. MySQL's `LIMIT` clause works hand-in-hand with sorting to restrict the number of rows returned by a query. For example, if you want to retrieve the top 10 customers with the highest total purchases, you can use the following query: `SELECT name, total_purchase FROM customers ORDER BY total_purchase DESC LIMIT 10;`. This query will return the top 10 customers sorted by their total purchase in descending order. The `LIMIT` clause is especially helpful when working with large datasets, as it allows you to narrow down the results to the most relevant rows.

Another useful feature when dealing with large datasets is pagination, which allows you to break the result set into smaller, more manageable chunks. Pagination typically involves two components: limiting the number of rows and skipping a specified number of rows before returning the result. MySQL's `LIMIT` and `OFFSET` clauses allow you to implement pagination. For example, if you want to retrieve the second page of 10 records from a table, you can use: `SELECT * FROM customers ORDER BY name ASC LIMIT 10 OFFSET 10;`. This will return records 11 through 20 in alphabetical order. Pagination is particularly useful when working with web applications or any interface that requires displaying large amounts of data across multiple pages.

When filtering and sorting data, it's important to be aware of the performance implications, especially when working with large datasets. Sorting and filtering without indexes can significantly slow down query performance, particularly when using `ORDER BY` or `WHERE` with large text fields or numerical data. MySQL uses indexes to quickly locate rows, which is why indexing columns frequently used in filtering or sorting can improve query performance. For example, if you regularly filter on the `city` column and sort results by `total_purchase`, you can create indexes on those columns: `CREATE INDEX idx_city ON customers(city); CREATE INDEX idx_total_purchase ON customers(total_purchase);`. Indexing the relevant columns can drastically improve query execution time, especially on large tables.

Filtering and sorting data also become more powerful when combined with aggregate functions, such as `COUNT()`, `SUM()`, `AVG()`, `MAX()`, and `MIN()`. You can filter and sort the results of aggregated data to perform meaningful analysis. For example, if you want to know the total sales for each product and sort them by total sales in descending order, you can write: `SELECT` product_id, SUM(sales_amount) AS total_sales FROM sales GROUP BY product_id ORDER BY total_sales DESC;. This query groups the sales data by product, sums the sales_amount for each group, and sorts the results by the total sales in descending order. By combining filtering, sorting, and aggregation, you can create powerful insights from your data.

One advanced technique when filtering and sorting is the use of window functions, which allow you to perform calculations across sets of rows related to the current row. For example, if you want to calculate the rank of each employee based on their total sales, you could use a window function like RANK(). An example query might look like this: SELECT name, total_sales, RANK() OVER (ORDER BY total_sales DESC) AS sales_rank FROM employees;. This query calculates the rank of each employee, ordered by total_sales in descending order. Window functions can provide advanced analytics and are especially useful when you need to calculate rankings, running totals, or moving averages. They provide a way to do these calculations while still preserving the individual rows of data.

To conclude, filtering and sorting are two of the most important SQL operations you'll use regularly in MySQL. In this chapter, we have covered the essentials of using the WHERE and ORDER BY clauses, as well as advanced techniques such as pagination, filtering by date, working with NULL values, and combining filtering and sorting with aggregate functions. By mastering these tools, you will be able to write powerful queries that retrieve only the data you need, organized in the way that best suits your analysis. In the next chapter, we will explore more advanced techniques, such as joining multiple tables and using subqueries to perform more complex data retrieval and manipulation tasks. Keep practicing with the queries and techniques discussed here to enhance your ability to work with MySQL and extract meaningful insights from your data.

Chapter 8: Introduction to SQL Joins in MySQL

1. One of the most powerful features of SQL is its ability to combine data from multiple tables using joins. In real-world databases, it's rare that all the data you need will be stored in a single table. Instead, data is typically divided across several tables, and relationships are established between those tables. The JOIN clause in SQL allows you to retrieve data from more than one table at the same time. In this chapter, we'll introduce you to the concept of SQL joins in MySQL, explaining how they work, the different types of joins, and how to use them to combine data from multiple tables. By the end of this chapter, you will be able to write SQL queries that retrieve and manipulate data from related tables effectively.

2. The primary purpose of a join is to combine rows from two or more tables based on a related column between them. Typically, this column is a foreign key in one table that references the primary key in another. The simplest example is joining two tables with a relationship between them, such as a customers table and an orders table. Each order is associated with a customer, so you can use a join to retrieve all orders along with

the customer information. The syntax for a basic `JOIN` is: `SELECT columns FROM table1 JOIN table2 ON table1.column = table2.column;`. This structure will be the foundation for all joins, and understanding it will allow you to expand to more complex queries.

3. The most common type of join is the `INNER JOIN`. An `INNER JOIN` returns only the rows that have matching values in both tables. For example, if you have a `customers` table and an `orders` table, you might want to retrieve a list of all customers who have made an order. The query would look like this: `SELECT customers.name, orders.order_id FROM customers INNER JOIN orders ON customers.id = orders.customer_id;`. This query returns only those customers who have placed an order. The `INNER JOIN` excludes any customers who do not have corresponding orders in the `orders` table.

4. An important feature of SQL joins is their ability to handle relationships between tables. In the example of the `customers` and `orders` tables, the `customer_id` in the `orders` table refers to the `id` column in the `customers` table. This type of relationship is known as a foreign key relationship. In SQL, you can join tables based on these relationships, ensuring that the data from the different tables aligns correctly. The ON clause in the join syntax specifies how the tables are related, typically matching the foreign key in one table to the primary key in another.

5. Sometimes, you may need to retrieve all rows from one table, even if there is no matching row in the other table. This is where `LEFT JOIN` (also known as `LEFT OUTER JOIN`) comes in. A `LEFT JOIN` returns all rows from the left table, and the matched rows from the right table. If there is no match, the result will include `NULL` for the right table's columns. For example, if you want to retrieve all customers and their corresponding orders, but include customers who haven't made any orders, you would write: `SELECT customers.name, orders.order_id FROM customers LEFT JOIN orders ON customers.id = orders.customer_id;`. This query will return all customers, including those with no orders, with `NULL` in the `order_id` column for customers who haven't made any purchases.

6. Similarly, a `RIGHT JOIN` (or `RIGHT OUTER JOIN`) returns all rows from the right table, and the matching rows from the left table. If there's no match, the result will contain `NULL` values for the left table's columns. This is less common than `LEFT JOIN`, but it is useful in certain situations, especially when you want to ensure all rows from the right table are included. For example, to retrieve all orders and their associated customers (including orders that may not have customer details), you would write: `SELECT customers.name, orders.order_id FROM customers RIGHT JOIN orders ON customers.id =`

orders.customer_id;. This will return all orders, including those that don't have an associated customer, with NULL in the name column for those orders.

7. Another type of join is the FULL OUTER JOIN, which returns all rows from both tables, with NULL values in columns where there is no match. However, MySQL does not natively support FULL OUTER JOIN. Instead, you can achieve the same result by combining a LEFT JOIN and a RIGHT JOIN with a UNION. For example, to retrieve all customers and all orders, including those without a match, you can use: SELECT customers.name, orders.order_id FROM customers LEFT JOIN orders ON customers.id = orders.customer_id UNION SELECT customers.name, orders.order_id FROM customers RIGHT JOIN orders ON customers.id = orders.customer_id;. This will return all rows from both the customers and orders tables, with NULL values where no match exists.

8. One of the more advanced types of joins is the SELF JOIN. A self join is a join where a table is joined with itself. This is useful when you need to compare rows within the same table. For example, suppose you have an employees table, where each employee has a manager_id that references the id of their manager in the same table. To retrieve the employee names and their managers, you would write: SELECT e.name AS employee, m.name AS manager FROM employees e LEFT JOIN employees m ON e.manager_id = m.id;. Here, the employees table is aliased twice—once as e for employees and once as m for managers—to perform the join within the same table.

9. Joining tables can sometimes return a lot of data, especially if you have many rows in the tables you are joining. It's important to be mindful of the efficiency of your joins, especially in large databases. Proper indexing on columns involved in joins (typically foreign keys and primary keys) can help speed up query performance. For example, if you are frequently joining the orders table with the customers table based on customer_id, make sure there is an index on the customer_id column in both tables. Indexes improve the speed at which MySQL can find matching rows during a join operation.

10. In some cases, you may need to join tables based on more than one condition. You can achieve this by adding multiple conditions to the ON clause. For example, if you want to retrieve orders for a specific product category and within a certain price range, you can write: SELECT orders.order_id, orders.total_amount, products.name FROM orders INNER JOIN products ON orders.product_id = products.id AND products.category = 'Electronics' AND orders.total_amount > 100;. This query joins the orders and products tables based on both the product_id and additional

conditions, such as product category and order price. By combining multiple conditions, you can refine your joins and ensure that only the most relevant data is returned.

11. Another important concept to understand is the concept of joining on more than one table. Often, your queries will need to retrieve data from three or more related tables. For example, if you want to retrieve the names of customers, their orders, and the products they've purchased, you might join the `customers`, `orders`, and `products` tables. The query would look something like this: `SELECT customers.name, orders.order_id, products.name FROM customers INNER JOIN orders ON customers.id = orders.customer_id INNER JOIN products ON orders.product_id = products.id;`. This query joins three tables—`customers`, `orders`, and `products`—to retrieve the desired data in a single result set. As the number of tables in a join increases, the complexity of the query can also increase, so it's important to be mindful of the relationships between your tables.

12. As you start to use joins more frequently, you may also want to explore advanced filtering options when working with multiple tables. In addition to using `WHERE` and `ON` clauses to filter the data, you can also use `HAVING` to filter data after grouping results. The `HAVING` clause is used to filter the results of aggregate functions and is often used with `GROUP BY` in complex queries. For example, to find customers who have spent more than $1000, you could write: `SELECT customers.name, SUM(orders.total_amount) AS total_spent FROM customers INNER JOIN orders ON customers.id = orders.customer_id GROUP BY customers.name HAVING total_spent > 1000;`. The `HAVING` clause filters the results after the `SUM` function has been applied, ensuring that only customers who have spent more than $1000 are returned.

13. Mastering SQL joins is crucial for working with relational databases effectively. Joins allow you to combine data from multiple tables and retrieve more complex, meaningful results. In this chapter, we have covered the different types of joins—`INNER JOIN`, `LEFT JOIN`, `RIGHT JOIN`, and `SELF JOIN`—and how to use them to combine related data. You've learned how to handle more complex join scenarios, such as joining on multiple conditions or combining several tables in a query. By practicing these techniques and understanding how joins work, you will be able to write more advanced SQL queries and retrieve data from multiple related tables with ease.

14. In conclusion, SQL joins are one of the most powerful and flexible tools in MySQL. They allow you to create complex queries that can combine and manipulate data from multiple tables. As you work with larger and more complex databases, understanding how to use joins effectively will be key to writing efficient queries that return the right data. In the next chapter, we will explore subqueries, which allow you to perform more advanced data retrieval and manipulation by embedding one query inside another. By mastering joins and subqueries, you will be well-equipped to handle even the most complex

database queries. Keep practicing with joins, and soon you'll be able to write sophisticated SQL queries with ease!

As you continue working with SQL joins in MySQL, it's important to remember that the choice of join can have a significant impact on the result set you receive. In particular, when you choose a `LEFT JOIN` or `RIGHT JOIN`, the result will contain more rows than with an `INNER JOIN`, especially when rows in one table don't have corresponding matches in the other. This is why understanding the business logic and relationships between the tables you are joining is essential. For example, if you are joining a `products` table with an `orders` table, but not all products have been ordered, using a `LEFT JOIN` will ensure that you still get all products listed in the result, with `NULL` values in the order details for those products that haven't been ordered.

Another key factor to consider when working with joins is the performance of your queries. Joins, especially on large tables, can sometimes be slow if not optimized correctly. To improve the performance of your join queries, you can use indexing. Indexing the columns you are joining on, such as primary and foreign keys, can significantly reduce query execution time by allowing MySQL to quickly find matching rows in each table. For example, if you frequently join the `orders` table with the `customers` table based on `customer_id`, creating an index on the `customer_id` column in both tables will speed up the join operation. Be mindful of indexing, though, as adding too many indexes can slow down `INSERT`, `UPDATE`, and `DELETE` operations, so it's important to find a balance that suits your needs.

It's also important to keep in mind that joining large tables or multiple tables can result in a huge result set, which may cause memory and performance issues. In such cases, using pagination can help you work with a manageable subset of data. Pagination involves limiting the number of rows returned by the query and displaying the data across multiple pages. MySQL's `LIMIT` and `OFFSET` clauses are used to implement pagination, as we discussed in Chapter 7. For example, if you are joining the `orders` and `products` tables and only want to retrieve the first 10 records, you can use: `SELECT * FROM orders INNER JOIN products ON orders.product_id = products.id LIMIT 10;`. You can also adjust the `OFFSET` to retrieve subsequent pages of data, for example: `SELECT * FROM orders INNER JOIN products ON orders.product_id = products.id LIMIT 10 OFFSET 10;`. Pagination is an effective way to prevent overwhelming the user or the system with too much data at once.

When performing joins with multiple tables, you may encounter situations where some rows are missing from the result set because of the type of join used. For instance, if you use an `INNER JOIN` between the `customers` and `orders` tables, only customers with corresponding orders will appear. However, if you want to include customers who haven't placed any orders, you would need to use a `LEFT JOIN`. It's important to understand these subtleties, as they can affect how your data is presented, especially in reporting or analysis tasks. In many cases, the choice of join type depends on the goal of your query. Do you want all records from one table and matched records from another, or do you only want the rows that have matching data in both tables? Understanding these choices will allow you to tailor your queries to the specific needs of your application or analysis.

As you work with joins, you may also encounter the need to join tables based on multiple columns. In situations where two or more columns are involved in establishing the relationship between tables, you can combine conditions in the ON clause of the join. For example, if you need to join the `employees` table with the `departments` table based on both `department_id` and `location_id`, you could write: `SELECT employees.name, departments.department_name FROM employees INNER JOIN departments ON employees.department_id = departments.id AND employees.location_id = departments.location_id;`. This query uses multiple conditions to ensure that both the `department_id` and `location_id` match in both tables. Joining on multiple columns can be helpful when the relationship between the tables is more complex and involves more than one key.

As you grow more experienced with joins, you'll also start using subqueries in combination with joins for even more powerful queries. A subquery is a query embedded within another query, and it can return data that is then used by the outer query. For example, if you want to find all customers who have placed orders above the average order value, you could use a subquery within a join like this: `SELECT customers.name, orders.order_id FROM customers INNER JOIN orders ON customers.id = orders.customer_id WHERE orders.total_amount > (SELECT AVG(total_amount) FROM orders);`. This query uses a subquery to calculate the average order amount and then returns all customers whose orders exceed that average. Subqueries can be very useful when you need to perform complex calculations or comparisons on your data before performing a join.

When dealing with multiple joins, it's essential to keep track of the table aliases and ensure that your queries are clear and readable. Using aliases for table names makes the query more concise, especially when you are joining several tables. For example, if you're joining three tables—`employees`, `departments`, and `projects`—using aliases like `e`, `d`, and `p` can make the query easier to read and maintain: `SELECT e.name AS employee_name, d.name AS department_name, p.name AS project_name FROM employees AS e INNER JOIN departments AS d ON e.department_id = d.id INNER JOIN projects AS p ON d.id = p.department_id;`. The use of table aliases helps prevent confusion when referencing columns from different tables, especially when the column names are the same across tables (e.g., `id` or `name` columns). Always strive to make your joins as clear and readable as possible to improve maintainability.

As you begin to create more complex queries with joins, it's crucial to test them thoroughly. Sometimes, subtle mistakes in join conditions can result in incorrect or unexpected results. For example, failing to properly match the foreign key column to the primary key column, or incorrectly using an `INNER JOIN` when a `LEFT JOIN` is needed, can lead to incomplete or misleading data. Always review your queries carefully, especially when working with multiple joins and subqueries, to ensure that they are returning the correct results.

To summarize, joins are a critical part of working with relational databases, and mastering the different types of joins will allow you to combine data from multiple tables efficiently. In this chapter, we introduced the `INNER JOIN`, `LEFT JOIN`, `RIGHT JOIN`, and `SELF JOIN` clauses, as well as the concept of joining on multiple columns and using subqueries with joins. We also discussed performance considerations, pagination, and best practices for writing clean, readable queries. By practicing these techniques and understanding how joins work, you'll be able to write sophisticated SQL queries that combine data from multiple sources and help you derive meaningful insights from your database.

As you continue to work with joins, keep experimenting with different types of joins and conditions to develop a deeper understanding of how they can be used to solve various data retrieval problems. Join operations are essential for any database-driven application, and mastering them will significantly enhance your ability to work with MySQL efficiently. In the next chapter, we will dive into advanced querying techniques, such as using subqueries for more complex filtering, grouping, and data manipulation. With a solid understanding of joins, you'll be well-prepared to tackle even the most complex data queries with confidence.

In conclusion, SQL joins are essential tools for combining and working with data stored in multiple tables. By learning how to use different types of joins, handle complex relationships, and optimize query performance, you will be able to unlock the full power of relational databases. Keep practicing with the examples provided in this chapter, and soon you'll be writing more complex queries that can handle sophisticated data needs. Your growing expertise with joins will set the stage for mastering even more advanced SQL topics, allowing you to perform powerful data analysis and reporting tasks.

Chapter 9: Grouping and Aggregating Data in MySQL

1. In this chapter, we will explore two of the most powerful operations in SQL: grouping and aggregating data. When working with large datasets, it's often necessary to summarize data to gain insights, such as calculating totals, averages, or counts. The ability to group data and apply aggregate functions is essential for performing analysis in MySQL. Grouping data allows you to organize it based on specific criteria, while aggregation enables you to perform calculations on each group. By the end of this chapter, you will understand how to use the `GROUP BY` clause and aggregate functions like `COUNT()`, `SUM()`, `AVG()`, `MIN()`, and `MAX()` to group and summarize data in meaningful ways.

2. The `GROUP BY` clause in SQL is used to group rows that have the same values in specified columns into summary rows. It is often used with aggregate functions to calculate a value for each group. The basic syntax for a query with `GROUP BY` is: `SELECT column1, aggregate_function(column2) FROM table_name GROUP BY column1;`. For example, if you have a `sales` table

and you want to know the total sales per product, you would write: `SELECT product_id, SUM(sales_amount) FROM sales GROUP BY product_id;`. This query groups the data by `product_id` and calculates the total sales for each product using the `SUM()` function. The `GROUP BY` clause ensures that the result is one row per product.

3. The `GROUP BY` clause can be used with multiple columns to group data by more than one criterion. For example, if you want to group sales by both product and year, you can write: `SELECT product_id, YEAR(sale_date) AS sale_year, SUM(sales_amount) FROM sales GROUP BY product_id, sale_year;`. This query groups the data first by `product_id`, then by the year extracted from the `sale_date`, and calculates the total sales for each group. You can group by as many columns as needed, making this a flexible tool for summarizing your data by multiple dimensions.

4. While grouping data, you can apply aggregate functions to calculate summary statistics for each group. MySQL supports several aggregate functions, such as `COUNT()`, `SUM()`, `AVG()`, `MIN()`, and `MAX()`. These functions allow you to perform calculations on a set of rows and return a single value. For example, if you want to count the number of orders for each customer, you can use the `COUNT()` function: `SELECT customer_id, COUNT(order_id) FROM orders GROUP BY customer_id;`. This query groups the data by `customer_id` and returns the total number of orders for each customer. Similarly, you can use the `SUM()` function to calculate the total sales for each product, `AVG()` to find the average order amount, or `MIN()` and `MAX()` to find the smallest and largest values, respectively, within each group.

5. The `COUNT()` function is one of the most commonly used aggregate functions in SQL. It returns the number of rows in a group. For example, if you want to know how many employees work in each department, you could use: `SELECT department_id, COUNT(*) FROM employees GROUP BY department_id;`. This query counts the number of employees in each department. The `*` inside the `COUNT()` function means it counts all rows within each group, even if some columns contain `NULL` values. If you want to count only non-`NULL` values in a specific column, you can specify the column name inside the `COUNT()` function, such as `COUNT(salary)` to count only non-null salary entries.

6. The `SUM()` function calculates the total sum of a numeric column in each group. For example, if you want to calculate the total sales per product, you would use: `SELECT product_id, SUM(sales_amount) FROM sales GROUP BY product_id;`. This query sums the `sales_amount` for each product and returns

the total sales for each group. The `SUM()` function is commonly used for calculating totals, such as total revenue, total orders, or total purchases.

7. The `AVG()` function calculates the average of a numeric column in each group. For example, if you want to know the average salary of employees in each department, you could write: `SELECT department_id, AVG(salary) FROM employees GROUP BY department_id;`. This query calculates the average salary for each department. The `AVG()` function is useful for finding means, such as the average score, average price, or average amount spent.

8. The `MIN()` and `MAX()` functions return the smallest and largest values, respectively, for a specific column in each group. For example, if you want to find the highest and lowest order amounts for each customer, you can write: `SELECT customer_id, MIN(order_amount), MAX(order_amount) FROM orders GROUP BY customer_id;`. This query returns the lowest and highest order amounts for each customer. The `MIN()` and `MAX()` functions are especially helpful when you want to find outliers or extremes within your data.

9. While the `GROUP BY` clause is powerful for summarizing data, sometimes you may want to filter the grouped results based on certain conditions. The `HAVING` clause is used to filter the results after the data has been grouped and aggregated. This is similar to the `WHERE` clause, but `WHERE` filters rows before grouping, while `HAVING` filters groups after they've been created. For example, if you want to find departments with more than 5 employees, you could write: `SELECT department_id, COUNT(*) FROM employees GROUP BY department_id HAVING COUNT(*) > 5;`. This query first groups employees by department, counts the number of employees in each department, and then filters out departments with 5 or fewer employees.

10. The `HAVING` clause is particularly useful when working with aggregate functions because you can apply conditions to the results of calculations, not just the raw data. For example, if you want to find products with total sales greater than $10,000, you can write: `SELECT product_id, SUM(sales_amount) FROM sales GROUP BY product_id HAVING SUM(sales_amount) > 10000;`. This query calculates the total sales for each product and then filters out products that have sales totals of $10,000 or less.

11. When working with `GROUP BY` and aggregate functions, it's important to remember that all non-aggregated columns in the `SELECT` statement must appear in the `GROUP BY` clause. For example, the following query will result in an error: `SELECT product_id, sales_amount, SUM(sales_amount) FROM sales GROUP BY product_id;`. This query is invalid because `sales_amount` is not part of an aggregate function and is not included in the `GROUP BY` clause. To fix this,

you would either need to aggregate sales_amount or include it in the GROUP BY clause: SELECT product_id, SUM(sales_amount) FROM sales GROUP BY product_id;. This ensures the query follows the proper rules for grouping and aggregation.

12. The GROUP BY clause can also be combined with ORDER BY to sort the results of your grouped data. For example, if you want to find the total sales per product and order the results from highest to lowest sales, you could write: SELECT product_id, SUM(sales_amount) FROM sales GROUP BY product_id ORDER BY SUM(sales_amount) DESC;. This query groups the sales by product, sums the sales for each product, and then orders the results in descending order based on the total sales amount.

13. You can also use GROUP BY with date and time data. For example, if you want to see the total sales for each month, you can group the data by month using MySQL's MONTH() function: SELECT MONTH(order_date) AS month, SUM(sales_amount) FROM sales GROUP BY MONTH(order_date);. This query groups sales by month and calculates the total sales for each month. You can use other date functions such as YEAR(), DAY(), and WEEK() to group data by different date parts, allowing for detailed time-based analysis.

14. While grouping and aggregation are incredibly useful, you should also be mindful of performance when working with large datasets. Grouping data can be resource-intensive, especially when using complex aggregate functions or when working with tables that contain millions of rows. To improve performance, you can index columns used in the GROUP BY clause and aggregate functions, such as primary keys and foreign keys, to speed up the process. It's also a good practice to filter data before grouping, using the WHERE clause to reduce the dataset as much as possible before applying GROUP BY.

15. In conclusion, grouping and aggregating data are essential tools for analyzing and summarizing large datasets in MySQL. The GROUP BY clause allows you to organize data into meaningful groups, while aggregate functions like COUNT(), SUM(), AVG(), MIN(), and MAX() enable you to calculate summary statistics for each group. The HAVING clause lets you filter groups based on aggregated data, while ORDER BY helps you sort the results. By mastering these tools, you'll be able to perform powerful data analysis and gain valuable insights from your database. In the next chapter, we will explore more advanced querying techniques, such as using subqueries and joins in combination with grouping and aggregation. Keep practicing with these concepts, and you'll soon be able to handle even the most complex data analysis tasks in MySQL.

As you become more comfortable with grouping and aggregating data, you may need to deal with more advanced aggregation techniques. One such technique is the use of **window functions**, which allow you to perform aggregate calculations over a specified range of rows that are related to the current row. These functions, like ROW_NUMBER(), RANK(), and SUM()

OVER(), can be used to calculate running totals or ranks while retaining the individual rows in the result set. For example, if you wanted to rank employees based on their sales, you could write: SELECT employee_id, total_sales, RANK() OVER (ORDER BY total_sales DESC) AS sales_rank FROM employees;. This query calculates the rank of each employee by their total sales without grouping the results. Window functions are incredibly powerful for situations where you need to retain the original row-level data but also want to perform aggregation over partitions of data.

Multi-level aggregation is another advanced feature that you may encounter when grouping data in MySQL. For example, you may want to calculate the total sales per product category and then within that, calculate the average sale amount for each product. This requires multiple levels of aggregation. You can achieve this by using nested queries. For example: SELECT category_id, SUM(sales_amount), AVG(sales_amount) FROM (SELECT category_id, sales_amount FROM products INNER JOIN sales ON products.product_id = sales.product_id) AS subquery GROUP BY category_id;. This query first selects the necessary data and then performs aggregation in an outer query, which is a technique often used when dealing with more complex business logic.

Sometimes, you may want to create **conditional aggregations** where you perform aggregations based on specific conditions or criteria. For example, if you want to calculate the total sales for each product but only for orders placed in the last 30 days, you can use the CASE statement within your aggregate function: SELECT product_id, SUM(CASE WHEN order_date >= CURDATE() - INTERVAL 30 DAY THEN sales_amount ELSE 0 END) AS recent_sales FROM sales GROUP BY product_id;. This query sums the sales amount for each product but only considers sales within the last 30 days. The CASE statement acts as a conditional filter, allowing you to apply aggregation based on dynamic conditions.

When performing aggregation, you may also want to handle **null values** in specific ways. By default, aggregate functions like SUM() and AVG() ignore NULL values, but you can manipulate them as needed. For example, if you want to include NULL values as zero in your aggregation, you can use the COALESCE() function to replace NULL with a specified value. Here's an example of counting orders, treating any missing values as zero: SELECT product_id, COUNT(COALESCE(order_id, 0)) FROM orders GROUP BY product_id;. This query will count NULL values in the order_id column as zeros, allowing them to be included in the aggregate calculation.

Grouping by expressions is another powerful feature in MySQL that allows you to group your data by more complex expressions rather than just a single column. For instance, you might want to group your sales data by month and year, even if your data includes specific dates. You can use MySQL's date functions to achieve this. For example: SELECT YEAR(order_date) AS order_year, MONTH(order_date) AS order_month,

`SUM(sales_amount) FROM sales GROUP BY YEAR(order_date), MONTH(order_date);`. This query groups the data by year and month and sums the sales amounts for each month. Grouping by expressions like this allows you to organize your data in more meaningful ways that go beyond simple column-based grouping.

As your queries become more complex, it's important to keep your code readable and maintainable. When working with grouping and aggregation, using **table aliases** and **descriptive column names** can greatly improve the clarity of your queries. For example, instead of using generic names like `SUM(sales_amount)`, use more descriptive aliases like `total_sales` to clarify the purpose of the aggregation. A well-organized query could look like this: `SELECT p.product_name, c.category_name, SUM(s.sales_amount) AS total_sales FROM sales s INNER JOIN products p ON s.product_id = p.product_id INNER JOIN categories c ON p.category_id = c.category_id GROUP BY p.product_name, c.category_name ORDER BY total_sales DESC;`. By clearly labeling the columns and using aliases for tables, the query becomes easier to read and understand, particularly when working with multiple joins and complex aggregations.

Having vs. Where: One of the most common points of confusion when grouping and aggregating data is the difference between `WHERE` and `HAVING` clauses. While both can be used to filter data, they serve different purposes. The `WHERE` clause filters rows before the data is grouped, while the `HAVING` clause filters after the data has been grouped and aggregated. For example, if you want to find products that have more than 10 orders in total, you could write: `SELECT product_id, COUNT(order_id) FROM orders GROUP BY product_id HAVING COUNT(order_id) > 10;`. In this case, the `HAVING` clause is used because you're filtering based on the aggregated count of orders, which happens after the grouping. If you were filtering based on individual rows, you would use the `WHERE` clause instead.

As you gain more experience with grouping and aggregation, you will encounter scenarios where you need to work with **subqueries**. Subqueries allow you to perform aggregations within a query and use the result in another part of the query. For example, you might want to select customers whose total spending exceeds the average total spending. You could use a subquery to calculate the average and then filter the customers using that value: `SELECT customer_id, SUM(total_purchase) FROM orders GROUP BY customer_id HAVING SUM(total_purchase) > (SELECT AVG(total_purchase) FROM orders);`. This query retrieves customers who have spent more than the average amount across all customers. Subqueries are extremely useful for more complex aggregations where the result of one query informs the filtering of another.

One more powerful tool to add to your aggregation toolkit is **distinct aggregation**. When you want to calculate an aggregate value but only include unique values in the calculation, you can use the `DISTINCT` keyword inside the aggregate function. For example, if you want to find the number of distinct customers who made purchases above $100, you would write: `SELECT COUNT(DISTINCT customer_id) FROM orders WHERE total_purchase > 100;`. This query counts only the distinct `customer_id` values, ensuring that duplicate entries for customers who made multiple purchases are not counted multiple times.

In conclusion, grouping and aggregating data are powerful techniques that allow you to summarize and analyze large datasets. In this chapter, we've explored how to use the `GROUP BY` clause to group data, along with various aggregate functions like `COUNT()`, `SUM()`, `AVG()`, `MIN()`, and `MAX()` to perform calculations on grouped data. We've also discussed advanced techniques like the `HAVING` clause, conditional aggregation, working with date functions, and optimizing query performance with window functions. By mastering these techniques, you'll be able to perform more complex data analysis and gain valuable insights from your MySQL databases. In the next chapter, we will explore subqueries and how they can be combined with grouping and aggregation for even more powerful querying capabilities. Keep practicing with these aggregation techniques to enhance your skills and become more proficient in SQL.

Chapter 10: Subqueries and Nested Queries in MySQL

1. In this chapter, we will explore one of the most powerful and flexible tools in SQL: **subqueries**. A subquery is a query within another query. It allows you to perform operations that would be difficult or impossible with a single query alone. Subqueries are commonly used to filter data based on the result of another query, to perform calculations on a subset of data, or to retrieve data for use in other queries. By the end of this chapter, you will understand how to use subqueries and nested queries effectively to make your MySQL queries more powerful and flexible.

2. A **subquery** is a query that is embedded inside another query. The subquery can be used in various parts of the main query, such as in the `SELECT`, `FROM`, or `WHERE` clauses. The basic syntax for a subquery is: `SELECT column1, column2 FROM table_name WHERE column1 IN (SELECT column1 FROM table_name WHERE condition);`. Here, the subquery is inside the `IN` clause and provides a list of values that the main query uses to filter the data. Subqueries are executed first, and the result is used by the main query to complete its execution.

3. One of the most common uses of subqueries is in the **WHERE** clause, where they are used to filter rows based on the result of another query. For example, suppose you want to retrieve customers who have spent more than the average amount in your store. You can use a subquery to calculate the average amount spent, and then use that result to filter the customers: `SELECT customer_id, total_purchase FROM orders WHERE total_purchase > (SELECT AVG(total_purchase) FROM orders);`. In this query, the subquery calculates the average purchase amount from the `orders` table, and the main query retrieves all customers who spent more than that

average. Subqueries in the `WHERE` clause are very useful when you need to filter data based on aggregate functions or comparisons to other datasets.

4. Subqueries can also be used in the **SELECT** clause to retrieve additional information for each row returned by the main query. For example, if you want to list customers along with the number of orders they have placed, you can write: `SELECT customer_id, (SELECT COUNT(*) FROM orders WHERE orders.customer_id = customers.customer_id) AS order_count FROM customers;`. In this query, the subquery is used to count the number of orders for each customer. The result of the subquery is returned as a new column called `order_count`. This is useful for adding calculated data to your result set without having to join tables or write complex calculations.

5. Another important use of subqueries is in the **FROM** clause, where the result of the subquery is treated as a temporary table or derived table. This is particularly useful when you want to perform multiple operations on the result of a query. For example, suppose you want to find the top 5 products by total sales, but only for orders placed in the last 30 days. You could use a subquery in the `FROM` clause to first filter the data and then calculate the total sales: `SELECT product_id, SUM(sales_amount) AS total_sales FROM (SELECT product_id, sales_amount FROM sales WHERE order_date >= CURDATE() - INTERVAL 30 DAY) AS recent_sales GROUP BY product_id ORDER BY total_sales DESC LIMIT 5;`. The subquery filters the sales data to include only orders from the last 30 days, and then the outer query calculates the total sales for each product and returns the top 5.

6. **Correlated subqueries** are a special type of subquery where the inner query references columns from the outer query. This makes the subquery dependent on the outer query, meaning that the subquery is executed once for each row of the outer query. For example, if you want to find all products that have been ordered more times than the average number of orders, you can write: `SELECT product_id FROM products p WHERE (SELECT COUNT(*) FROM orders o WHERE o.product_id = p.product_id) > (SELECT AVG(order_count) FROM (SELECT COUNT(*) AS order_count FROM orders GROUP BY product_id) AS avg_orders);`. In this query, the subquery in the `WHERE` clause counts the number of orders for each product (based on the outer query's product ID), and then compares it to the average number of orders per product. Correlated subqueries are powerful, but they can be less efficient than non-correlated subqueries, so it's important to use them wisely.

7. Another type of subquery is the **scalar subquery**, which returns a single value (a single row and column). Scalar subqueries are often used in comparison operators such as =, <, >, or `IN`. For example, if you want to find customers whose total purchase is greater than the total sales of the product with the highest sales, you could write: `SELECT`

customer_id, total_purchase FROM orders WHERE total_purchase > (SELECT MAX(sales_amount) FROM sales);. The scalar subquery returns the maximum sales amount, and the outer query compares each customer's total purchase to this value.

8. **Subqueries in the IN clause** are also common. The IN operator is used when you want to compare a column value to a set of values, and a subquery can generate that set of values dynamically. For example, if you want to retrieve customers who have ordered a specific product, you could write: `SELECT customer_id FROM orders WHERE product_id IN (SELECT product_id FROM products WHERE category = 'Electronics');`. The subquery retrieves all product IDs for items in the "Electronics" category, and the outer query returns all customers who have ordered one of those products. Using subqueries with IN is helpful when you need to dynamically filter data based on another set of conditions.

9. **Subqueries with EXISTS** are used when you need to check for the existence of rows that meet certain criteria. The EXISTS operator returns true if the subquery returns any rows, and false if it returns no rows. For example, if you want to find customers who have placed orders for at least one product in the "Electronics" category, you could write: `SELECT customer_id FROM customers WHERE EXISTS (SELECT 1 FROM orders o JOIN products p ON o.product_id = p.product_id WHERE p.category = 'Electronics' AND o.customer_id = customers.customer_id);`. The subquery checks for the existence of orders for electronics products, and the outer query returns only those customers who have made such orders. The EXISTS operator is efficient because it stops executing the subquery as soon as it finds a matching row.

10. Subqueries can also be used for **data validation** in MySQL. For example, you can use a subquery to check if a value exists before allowing an operation to proceed. This is commonly used in INSERT, UPDATE, or DELETE statements. For example, you might want to ensure that a customer's email address is unique before inserting a new customer record. The query would look like: `INSERT INTO customers (name, email) SELECT 'John Doe', 'john.doe@example.com' WHERE NOT EXISTS (SELECT 1 FROM customers WHERE email = 'john.doe@example.com');`. This query inserts a new customer only if no customer with that email address already exists in the table.

11. **Nested subqueries** are subqueries that contain other subqueries. These can be useful for performing multiple levels of filtering or aggregation. For example, if you want to find products with total sales greater than the average sales of products in the "Electronics" category, you could write: SELECT product_id, SUM(sales_amount) FROM sales WHERE product_id IN (SELECT product_id FROM products WHERE category = 'Electronics' AND

sales_amount > (SELECT AVG(sales_amount) FROM products WHERE category = 'Electronics')) GROUP BY product_id;. In this query, the inner subquery calculates the average sales amount for products in the "Electronics" category, and the outer subquery uses that result to filter products with higher-than-average sales.

12. One of the most important things to keep in mind when working with subqueries is their performance. Subqueries, especially correlated subqueries, can be computationally expensive because they may require MySQL to execute the subquery multiple times, once for each row in the outer query. It's important to analyze your queries carefully and, when possible, optimize them by using joins instead of subqueries. For example, rather than using a correlated subquery to count orders for each customer, you could use a JOIN to combine the data and calculate the count in a more efficient manner.

13. In conclusion, subqueries are a powerful feature of MySQL that allow you to embed one query within another, enabling you to filter, calculate, and manipulate data in more complex ways. In this chapter, we've covered various types of subqueries, including scalar subqueries, correlated subqueries, subqueries in the WHERE, SELECT, and FROM clauses, and subqueries with IN, EXISTS, and HAVING. You've learned how to use subqueries for data aggregation, conditional filtering, and data validation. While subqueries are highly useful, it's important to understand when to use them and when alternative techniques like joins might be more efficient. In the next chapter, we will explore further advanced SQL techniques for data manipulation, focusing on transactions, triggers, and stored procedures. Keep practicing with subqueries, and soon you'll be writing complex and efficient queries that handle sophisticated data retrieval tasks with ease.

14. As you work with subqueries, it's crucial to understand **performance implications**. While subqueries can be powerful, they may not always be the most efficient way to structure a query, especially when dealing with large datasets. In many cases, subqueries can lead to performance issues, particularly when they are executed for each row in the outer query. For instance, correlated subqueries are often slower than joins because they need to be evaluated multiple times—once for each row in the outer query. To optimize queries, you should consider alternative approaches, such as **joins** or **temporary tables**, where appropriate. These alternatives can improve performance, particularly when dealing with large amounts of data.

15. In some cases, **subqueries** can be replaced with **JOINs**. A JOIN often performs better than a subquery because it allows MySQL to scan the tables more efficiently. For example, instead of using a subquery to find the highest sales for each product, you can perform a JOIN to calculate the same result. Consider this query: SELECT products.product_name, MAX(sales.sales_amount) AS max_sales FROM products JOIN sales ON products.product_id = sales.product_id GROUP BY products.product_name;. This is more efficient than a subquery, as it avoids the need for nested queries and allows MySQL to handle the aggregation in one step. When performance is critical, especially on larger datasets, consider optimizing your queries by using joins instead of subqueries.

16. While subqueries offer a lot of flexibility, one of the **common pitfalls** is using subqueries in situations where joins would be more appropriate. For example, using subqueries to filter data based on values that exist in related tables can lead to inefficiencies. Instead of using a subquery to filter the customers who have placed orders, as in: `SELECT customer_id FROM customers WHERE customer_id IN (SELECT customer_id FROM orders);`, a more efficient approach would be to use an `INNER JOIN`: `SELECT customers.customer_id FROM customers INNER JOIN orders ON customers.customer_id = orders.customer_id;`. Joins tend to be more efficient because they work directly with the tables' indexes, while subqueries often result in the need for MySQL to evaluate the inner query repeatedly for each row in the outer query.

17. When working with **nested subqueries**, it's essential to maintain clarity and avoid overly complex queries. While nesting queries is useful in certain scenarios, it can make the SQL code harder to read and maintain. To improve readability and make debugging easier, break complex queries into simpler steps or use **Common Table Expressions** (CTEs) when possible. A CTE allows you to define a temporary result set that can be referenced within a larger query. In MySQL 8.0 and later, you can use CTEs like so: `WITH recent_sales AS ( SELECT product_id, SUM(sales_amount) AS total_sales FROM sales WHERE order_date >= CURDATE() - INTERVAL 30 DAY GROUP BY product_id ) SELECT p.product_name, r.total_sales FROM products p JOIN recent_sales r ON p.product_id = r.product_id;`. This CTE simplifies the logic by breaking it into two parts: first, calculating the recent sales, and then using that result in the main query. CTEs are especially helpful for improving readability when working with complex nested subqueries.

18. **Subqueries in the `HAVING` clause** are often used when performing aggregation and need to filter results based on the aggregated data. For instance, if you want to retrieve customers who have placed more than the average number of orders, you could write: `SELECT customer_id, COUNT(order_id) AS order_count FROM orders GROUP BY customer_id HAVING COUNT(order_id) > (SELECT AVG(order_count) FROM (SELECT COUNT(*) AS order_count FROM orders GROUP BY customer_id) AS avg_orders);`. In this case, the outer query groups the orders by `customer_id` and counts the number of orders, while the subquery calculates the average number of orders per customer. The `HAVING` clause then filters customers whose order count is

above the average. Subqueries in `HAVING` clauses allow you to filter data after the grouping and aggregation process.

19. While **subqueries in the `SELECT` clause** are not as commonly used as in the `WHERE` clause, they can still be very powerful. When you need to calculate values on a row-by-row basis, a subquery in the `SELECT` clause is helpful. For example, to calculate the total sales for each product, you could use: `SELECT product_id, (SELECT SUM(sales_amount) FROM sales WHERE sales.product_id = products.product_id) AS total_sales FROM products;`. Here, the subquery is used to calculate the sum of sales for each product. While this works, it's worth noting that for performance reasons, **JOINs** are often more efficient in such scenarios. However, when a single subquery is required for each row and there is no alternative, subqueries in the `SELECT` clause can still be a useful tool.

20. Another feature of subqueries is their ability to perform **data comparison**. This is particularly useful when you need to compare values across different datasets. For example, if you want to find employees who earn more than the average salary for their department, you can write: `SELECT employee_id, salary FROM employees WHERE salary > (SELECT AVG(salary) FROM employees WHERE department_id = employees.department_id);`. In this case, the subquery calculates the average salary for each department, and the outer query retrieves employees whose salaries exceed the department's average. This type of subquery is useful when comparing individual records to a value calculated from a different subset of data.

21. **Best practices** when working with subqueries include the following:

- Use subqueries when they simplify logic and improve the readability of your queries. However, avoid using subqueries when a `JOIN` can accomplish the same task more efficiently.

- Be cautious with correlated subqueries, as they can result in performance issues on large datasets due to multiple executions for each row in the outer query.

- Ensure your subqueries are properly optimized, especially when dealing with aggregate functions or complex filtering. Sometimes, breaking up a large query with subqueries into smaller queries or using CTEs can make the query more efficient and easier to understand.

- Always test your queries and monitor performance, especially if the queries are running on large datasets or are used frequently in your application.

22. To conclude, subqueries are a powerful tool that enables you to write more flexible, efficient, and complex queries in MySQL. In this chapter, you've learned how to use subqueries in various parts of a query, including the `WHERE`, `SELECT`, and `FROM`

clauses. You've also seen how to use correlated subqueries, scalar subqueries, and subqueries with `IN`, `EXISTS`, and `HAVING`. Subqueries provide a great deal of flexibility for filtering and aggregating data, but they should be used wisely, as they can sometimes lead to performance issues. Understanding when to use subqueries, when to opt for joins, and how to optimize your queries will make you a more efficient MySQL user. In the next chapter, we will explore advanced techniques for **transactions, triggers, and stored procedures**, which will allow you to manage complex database operations and ensure data integrity. Keep practicing with subqueries, and you'll be able to solve increasingly sophisticated data retrieval problems in MySQL.

Chapter 11: Introduction to Indexing in MySQL

1. In this chapter, we will explore one of the most important performance optimization techniques in MySQL: **indexing**. Indexing is a mechanism that allows MySQL to quickly locate rows in a table without scanning the entire table. It is especially useful when working with large datasets, as it can dramatically speed up the performance of queries that involve searching, sorting, or joining large tables. However, while indexes can improve query performance, they also come with trade-offs in terms of storage space and write performance. By the end of this chapter, you will understand how indexes work, how to create them, and how to use them effectively to optimize your MySQL queries.

2. An **index** in MySQL is a data structure that improves the speed of data retrieval operations on a table. It works similarly to the index of a book, which allows you to quickly locate a specific topic without having to read the entire book. Indexes in MySQL are typically created on columns that are frequently used in search conditions, `JOIN` conditions, or `ORDER BY` clauses. When an index is created on a column, MySQL builds an internal structure that allows it to quickly find matching values, rather than having to scan every row in the table.

3. The most common type of index is the **B-tree index**, which is used by MySQL for most storage engines (including InnoDB and MyISAM). A B-tree index organizes the data in a way that allows MySQL to search for values efficiently using a tree-like structure. When you search for a value in a B-tree index, MySQL can quickly narrow down the possible locations of the value, much like a binary search. Other types of indexes include **hash indexes**, **spatial indexes**, and **full-text indexes**, but for most use cases, B-tree indexes will be the most relevant.

4. Indexes can be created on one or more columns, and the type of index you choose depends on how the indexed columns are used in queries. To create a simple index on a single column, you can use the `CREATE INDEX` statement. The basic syntax is: `CREATE INDEX index_name ON table_name (column_name);`. For example, if you have a `customers` table and want to create an index on the `email` column, you would write: `CREATE INDEX idx_email ON customers (email);`. This index allows MySQL to quickly look up customers by their email address, which is useful for queries that search for customers by email.

5. In addition to creating indexes manually, MySQL also automatically creates indexes for primary keys and unique constraints. When you define a primary key on a table, MySQL automatically creates a unique index on the primary key column(s). For example, if you create a table with a primary key on the `id` column, MySQL automatically creates an index on `id`. Similarly, when you define a `UNIQUE` constraint on a column, MySQL creates a unique index to enforce that no two rows in the table can have the same value for that column.

6. **Composite indexes** are indexes created on multiple columns. These indexes are useful when your queries filter on more than one column at a time. For example, if you frequently run queries that filter on both the `first_name` and `last_name` columns, you can create a composite index on both columns: `CREATE INDEX idx_name ON customers (first_name, last_name);`. This index helps MySQL quickly find rows that match both `first_name` and `last_name`. However, it's important to note that MySQL can only use the first column(s) of a composite index for queries that filter on those columns. For example, a composite index on `(first_name, last_name)` will be used for queries that filter on `first_name` and `last_name` together, but it won't be used effectively if you only filter by `last_name`.

7. **Unique indexes** are a type of index that enforces uniqueness on the values in a column. When you create a unique index on a column, MySQL ensures that all values in that column are distinct. This is useful for columns that must contain unique data, such as email addresses or usernames. The syntax for creating a unique index is similar to a regular index, but you use the `UNIQUE` keyword: `CREATE UNIQUE INDEX idx_unique_email ON customers (email);`. This will ensure that each email address in the `customers` table is unique.

8. **Full-text indexes** are specialized indexes used for text searching. These indexes allow you to search for words or phrases within text columns, making them particularly useful for searching large bodies of text, such as blog posts, articles, or product descriptions. Full-text indexes are only available in MySQL's `InnoDB` and `MyISAM` storage engines, and they work differently from regular B-tree indexes. You can create a full-text index on a text column using the following syntax: `CREATE FULLTEXT INDEX idx_fulltext_description ON products (description);`. Once the index is created, you can use the `MATCH()` and `AGAINST()` functions to perform full-text searches: `SELECT * FROM products WHERE MATCH(description) AGAINST('keyword');`. Full-text indexes are especially powerful for performing text searches that allow for more flexibility, such as finding similar words or phrases.

9. **Spatial indexes** are used for indexing spatial data types, such as geometrical shapes, locations, and coordinates. If you are working with geographic data, spatial indexes can improve the performance of queries that deal with spatial relationships, such as finding

nearby locations. For example, in MySQL, you might use a spatial index to speed up queries that calculate distances between points: `CREATE SPATIAL INDEX idx_location ON locations (coordinates);`. These indexes are used for specialized queries related to geospatial data and require specific data types like `POINT`, `LINESTRING`, or `POLYGON`.

10. One important concept to understand when working with indexes is **index maintenance**. Indexes help speed up queries, but they also add overhead to insert, update, and delete operations. When you insert a new row into a table, MySQL must also update any indexes that are affected by the insert. Similarly, when you delete a row or update an indexed column, MySQL must adjust the relevant indexes. This can lead to additional processing time, especially if you have many indexes on a table. It's important to strike a balance between query performance and write performance when deciding which indexes to create.

11. To avoid unnecessary overhead, it's a good practice to **drop indexes** that are not being used. MySQL provides the `DROP INDEX` statement to remove an index from a table. The syntax is: `DROP INDEX index_name ON table_name;`. For example, if you no longer need the index on the `email` column in the `customers` table, you can drop it using: `DROP INDEX idx_email ON customers;`. Periodically reviewing and dropping unused indexes will help maintain optimal performance for both read and write operations.

12. Another important aspect of index management is the **index cardinality**. Cardinality refers to the number of distinct values in a column. Indexes are more beneficial when they are applied to columns with high cardinality (i.e., columns with many distinct values), such as `email` or `customer_id`. Indexes on columns with low cardinality (i.e., columns with very few distinct values, such as boolean flags or categorical columns) may not provide significant performance improvements. In some cases, indexes on low-cardinality columns can even degrade performance, as MySQL may choose a full table scan over using the index. It's important to consider the cardinality of your columns when deciding whether to create an index.

13. **Index statistics** are valuable for MySQL's query optimizer to determine the most efficient execution plan for a query. MySQL collects statistics on each index, including the distribution of values and the size of the index. These statistics help MySQL decide which index to use for a query, ensuring that the most optimal query plan is chosen. However, sometimes the optimizer might choose a less efficient index. In such cases, you can use **EXPLAIN** to analyze your query and see how MySQL is using indexes: `EXPLAIN SELECT * FROM customers WHERE email = 'john.doe@example.com';`. This command shows you the execution plan and the indexes that MySQL uses for the query. If you notice that MySQL is not using the best index, you can consider adjusting the query or indexing strategy to improve performance.

14. **Covering indexes** are a powerful optimization technique where an index contains all the columns required for a query. This means that the database can satisfy the query entirely from the index, without needing to access the table data itself. For example, if you have a query that retrieves the `email` and `name` columns from the `customers` table and you create a composite index on `(email, name)`, MySQL can use this index to fulfill the query without needing to read the actual table rows: `CREATE INDEX idx_email_name ON customers (email, name);`. Covering indexes can drastically improve query performance by reducing disk I/O, especially for read-heavy applications.

15. In conclusion, indexing is a vital technique for optimizing query performance in MySQL. By creating the right indexes on frequently queried columns, you can significantly speed up data retrieval, especially for large datasets. In this chapter, we've covered the basics of creating and managing indexes, including B-tree indexes, composite indexes, unique indexes, full-text indexes, and spatial indexes. We also discussed the importance of balancing index creation with write performance and the need to periodically review and drop unused indexes. Understanding when and where to use indexes, along with optimizing index strategies based on query patterns, will make you more effective in managing MySQL performance. In the next chapter, we will explore more advanced topics related to **query optimization and performance tuning**, ensuring that your MySQL database remains fast and efficient as it grows. Keep practicing with indexing, and you'll soon be able to optimize even the most complex queries in MySQL!

16. **Index Compression** is another important consideration when working with large tables. Indexes, especially on large tables, can take up a significant amount of storage space. MySQL offers a method of compressing indexes to reduce their size, which can help save storage space and improve I/O performance. Compression is typically used with **InnoDB** tables, where the `KEY_BLOCK_SIZE` option can be set when creating a table or index. For example: `CREATE INDEX idx_name ON my_table (column_name) KEY_BLOCK_SIZE = 8;`. This will create an index with a block size of 8KB, reducing the amount of storage required for the index. While compression can be beneficial for large datasets, it's important to test its impact on performance, as there can be trade-offs in terms of write performance due to the extra processing required for compression and decompression.

17. **Multi-column indexes** are particularly useful when your queries involve conditions that filter on multiple columns. For example, if you have a query that filters based on both `first_name` and `last_name`, a composite index on both of those columns would be more efficient than creating separate indexes on each column. The syntax to create a multi-column index is: `CREATE INDEX idx_name ON table_name (column1, column2);`. For example: `CREATE INDEX idx_full_name ON employees (first_name, last_name);`. This index is used when queries filter on both `first_name` and `last_name`, which reduces the time it takes MySQL to search for rows matching those conditions. However, keep in mind that multi-column indexes are most effective when queries use the leftmost prefix of the index (i.e.,

columns that appear first in the index definition). For a composite index on `(first_name, last_name)`, a query filtering only by `last_name` may not use the index effectively.

18. **Covering indexes** are a highly useful optimization technique when you want to minimize the need for MySQL to access the table after using the index. A covering index includes all the columns required to satisfy the query in the index itself. This means MySQL can return the result from the index alone, without needing to read the table rows. For example, if you frequently run a query like: `SELECT email, first_name, last_name FROM customers WHERE email = 'john.doe@example.com';`, you could create a composite index that includes all the columns involved in the query: `CREATE INDEX idx_customer_email ON customers (email, first_name, last_name);`. This index would be considered a "covering index" because it contains all the columns needed to fulfill the query, and MySQL can return the result directly from the index, improving performance by avoiding extra disk access.

19. **Using EXPLAIN for Index Optimization** is an essential practice for understanding how MySQL uses indexes to execute queries. The `EXPLAIN` statement shows you the query execution plan, including how MySQL intends to retrieve data and which indexes it will use. By analyzing the output of `EXPLAIN`, you can determine if your queries are using the best possible indexes, or if there are performance bottlenecks that need to be addressed. For example, you can run: `EXPLAIN SELECT * FROM orders WHERE customer_id = 101;`. This will give you a detailed report on how MySQL plans to execute the query, whether it will use an index, and which index it is using. If the output shows a `SIMPLE` query type, but the `key` column is `NULL`, it indicates that no index is being used, and you may need to consider adding one for better performance.

20. **Partial Indexes** in MySQL can also be useful in cases where you want to index only a portion of a column's data. For example, if you have a `description` column with very long text values and often search for specific patterns at the beginning of the column, you can create a partial index to index only the first N characters of the column. The syntax for creating a partial index is as follows: `CREATE INDEX idx_partial_description ON products (description(255));`. This creates an index on the first 255 characters of the `description` column. Partial indexes are a good solution for large text fields where indexing the entire column would be inefficient or unnecessary.

21. **Indexing Strategies for Read vs. Write Operations**: When designing indexes, it's important to consider the trade-offs between **read performance** and **write performance**. While indexes significantly speed up read operations (SELECT queries), they introduce overhead for write operations (INSERT, UPDATE, and DELETE), as MySQL must update the indexes every time data is modified. For applications with heavy write

operations, it may be necessary to carefully select which indexes to create. For example, instead of indexing every column, focus on indexing columns that are frequently used in filtering, sorting, or joining operations. For heavy transactional systems, the key is balancing index creation with write performance.

22. **Monitoring Index Usage**: As your database grows, it's important to monitor the usage of your indexes to ensure that they are being used effectively. MySQL provides the `SHOW INDEX` statement to view information about indexes in a table: `SHOW INDEX FROM table_name;`. This query provides details such as the index name, the columns included in the index, whether the index is unique, and how many rows MySQL has examined using the index. Regularly reviewing this information can help you determine if there are any unused or underused indexes that could be dropped, freeing up storage and improving write performance.

23. **Removing Unused Indexes**: Over time, as the application evolves and query patterns change, some indexes may no longer be needed. Keeping unnecessary indexes can result in wasted disk space and slower write performance. If you determine that an index is no longer being used, it's important to drop it. You can do this with the `DROP INDEX` command: `DROP INDEX index_name ON table_name;`. Before removing an index, always analyze whether it's truly unused and verify that removing it won't negatively affect query performance.

24. **Best Practices for Indexing**:

- **Focus on High-Cardinality Columns**: Index columns with many unique values (high cardinality) because they benefit the most from indexing. For example, columns like `email`, `user_id`, or `product_id` are ideal candidates for indexing.

- **Use Composite Indexes Wisely**: When queries filter on multiple columns, consider using composite indexes. However, make sure to index the columns in the order they are typically queried, as the index's effectiveness depends on the column order.

- **Limit the Number of Indexes**: Too many indexes can degrade performance due to the overhead of maintaining them. Be selective about which indexes to create, and prioritize those that will improve query performance.

- **Regularly Review Indexes**: Periodically review the indexes in your database to ensure they are still useful and being utilized by queries. Removing unused indexes can improve write performance and free up storage.

25. **Conclusion**: Indexing is one of the most powerful tools for optimizing query performance in MySQL. By creating the right indexes on the right columns, you can speed up data retrieval, improve query efficiency, and enhance the overall performance of your database. In this chapter, we have covered the different types of indexes, including simple, composite, unique, full-text, and spatial indexes, and discussed strategies for creating, managing, and optimizing them. We've also explored best practices for

indexing, including considering the trade-offs between read and write performance and regularly reviewing index usage. Mastering indexing will allow you to write more efficient queries and handle larger datasets with ease. In the next chapter, we will dive into **query optimization** techniques, including tips and tricks for improving MySQL query performance beyond indexing. Keep experimenting with indexing and you'll soon become an expert in MySQL performance tuning!

Chapter 12: MySQL Functions for Beginners

1. In this chapter, we will introduce you to **MySQL functions**, which are essential tools for performing operations on data within MySQL. Functions are predefined operations that allow you to manipulate, format, and calculate data directly in your queries. They help streamline tasks like performing mathematical calculations, manipulating strings, working with dates, and converting data types. By the end of this chapter, you'll be familiar with the basic MySQL functions and understand how to use them to simplify your SQL queries and improve the efficiency of your data manipulation.

2. MySQL provides a wide variety of functions that can be categorized into different groups, such as **string functions**, **numeric functions**, **date and time functions**, **aggregate functions**, and **conversion functions**. Each group of functions is designed to perform specific operations on data types like text, numbers, dates, or even entire datasets. In this chapter, we will focus on some of the most commonly used functions across these categories, starting with the basics and building up to more complex uses.

3. **String Functions** are used to manipulate string data types. MySQL provides many string functions for operations like concatenating, finding lengths, and extracting portions of text. One of the simplest string functions is `CONCAT()`, which allows you to combine two or more strings together. For example, if you want to combine a customer's first and last name into a full name, you can write: `SELECT CONCAT(first_name, ' ', last_name) AS full_name FROM customers;`. This query concatenates the `first_name` and `last_name` columns, adding a space between them, and returns the result as `full_name`.

4. Another useful string function is `LENGTH()`, which returns the length of a string in characters. For example: `SELECT LENGTH('Hello World') AS string_length;`. This query returns `11` because "Hello World" contains 11 characters. The `LENGTH()` function is useful when you need to measure the size of text or ensure that a string meets certain length requirements.

5. If you need to find a specific substring within a string, you can use the `SUBSTRING()` function. This function allows you to extract a portion of a string. For example, to extract the first three characters of a customer's name, you would write: `SELECT SUBSTRING(name, 1, 3) AS first_three_chars FROM customers;`. This query returns the first three characters of each customer's name.

6. **Numeric Functions** perform operations on numeric data types, such as integers and decimals. One common numeric function is `ROUND()`, which rounds a number to a specified number of decimal places. For example, if you want to round the total price of an order to two decimal places, you would write: `SELECT ROUND(total_price, 2) AS rounded_price FROM orders;`. This query rounds the `total_price` column to two decimal places.

7. Another useful numeric function is `ABS()`, which returns the absolute value of a number. For instance, if you want to find the absolute difference between two values, you could write: `SELECT ABS(sale_price - cost_price) AS price_difference FROM products;`. This query calculates the absolute value of the difference between `sale_price` and `cost_price`, which is helpful when you need to ensure the result is always positive.

8. The `FLOOR()` and `CEIL()` (or `CEILING()`) functions are useful when you want to round numbers down or up, respectively. For example, to round the price of an item down to the nearest whole number, you would use: `SELECT FLOOR(price) AS rounded_down_price FROM items;`. This query returns the largest integer less than or equal to the value of `price`. Conversely, if you want to round a number up, use `CEIL()`: `SELECT CEIL(price) AS rounded_up_price FROM items;`.

9. **Date and Time Functions** are extremely useful for manipulating date and time data. MySQL has a wide variety of functions for extracting specific parts of dates, adding or subtracting time, and formatting date values. For example, the `NOW()` function returns the current date and time: `SELECT NOW() AS current_datetime;`. This query will return the current date and time in the format `YYYY-MM-DD HH:MM:SS`.

10. The `DATE()` function is used to extract the date part of a datetime value. For example, if you have a column that stores both the date and time of an order and you only want the date, you would write: `SELECT DATE(order_datetime) AS order_date FROM orders;`. This query will return only the date portion of the `order_datetime` column, ignoring the time.

11. Another useful date function is `DATEDIFF()`, which returns the difference between two dates. For example, to find out how many days have passed since an order was placed, you could use: `SELECT DATEDIFF(NOW(), order_date) AS days_since_order FROM orders;`. This query will return the number of days between the current date (`NOW()`) and the `order_date` column.

12. **Aggregate Functions** are used to perform calculations on a group of rows. These functions are essential for summarizing data, such as calculating totals, averages, and counts. Some of the most common aggregate functions include `COUNT()`, `SUM()`,

AVG(), MIN(), and MAX(). For example, to count the number of orders placed by each customer, you would write: `SELECT customer_id, COUNT(order_id) AS order_count FROM orders GROUP BY customer_id;`. This query counts the number of orders for each customer and groups the results by `customer_id`.

13. The SUM() function calculates the total sum of a numeric column. For example, to calculate the total sales for each product, you would write: `SELECT product_id, SUM(sales_amount) AS total_sales FROM sales GROUP BY product_id;`. This query sums the `sales_amount` for each `product_id` and returns the total sales for each product.

14. If you need to calculate the average value of a column, the AVG() function is used. For example, to calculate the average salary of employees in each department, you would write: `SELECT department_id, AVG(salary) AS average_salary FROM employees GROUP BY department_id;`. This query calculates the average salary for each department.

15. **Conversion Functions** are used to convert data from one data type to another. For example, the CAST() function can be used to explicitly convert one data type into another. For instance, to convert a string to an integer, you can use: `SELECT CAST('123' AS SIGNED) AS converted_value;`. This query converts the string '123' into an integer and returns 123 as the result.

16. The CONVERT() function is another way to change the data type of a value. For example, to convert a number to a string, you can use: `SELECT CONVERT(123, CHAR) AS converted_string;`. This converts the number 123 into a string '123'.

17. **NULL Handling Functions** are essential when working with missing or undefined data. For example, the IFNULL() function allows you to replace NULL values with a default value. For example: `SELECT IFNULL(commission, 0) AS commission_amount FROM sales;`. This query will return 0 for any rows where the `commission` column contains NULL, and the actual commission value otherwise.

18. The COALESCE() function is another useful way to handle NULL values. It returns the first non-NULL value from a list of expressions. For example: `SELECT COALESCE(phone_number, 'Not Available') AS contact_phone FROM customers;`. This query will return the customer's phone number if it is not NULL, and 'Not Available' if the phone number is NULL.

19. **Mathematical Functions** are also an important part of MySQL and can be used to perform mathematical operations directly in your queries. For example, the `POW()` function calculates the power of a number. To calculate the square of a number, you can write: `SELECT POW(5, 2) AS square_value;`. This will return `25` as the square of `5`.

20. In conclusion, MySQL functions are a powerful way to manipulate and calculate data directly within your queries. Whether you're working with strings, numbers, dates, or handling `NULL` values, understanding how to use MySQL functions will make your queries more efficient and versatile. In this chapter, we've covered some of the most commonly used functions for beginners, including string, numeric, date and time, aggregate, and conversion functions. These functions can be combined in powerful ways to create more sophisticated queries. In the next chapter, we will dive deeper into **advanced MySQL functions** and explore how to use them to solve more complex data problems. Keep experimenting with these functions, and you'll soon become proficient in data manipulation in MySQL!

21. **String Functions Continued**: In addition to the functions we've discussed, MySQL provides several other string functions for more advanced string manipulation. The `REPLACE()` function, for instance, allows you to replace all occurrences of a substring within a string. For example: `SELECT REPLACE('Hello World', 'World', 'MySQL') AS new_string;`. This will return `'Hello MySQL'`, as the function replaces "World" with "MySQL" in the string `'Hello World'`.

22. Another useful string function is `TRIM()`, which removes leading and trailing spaces from a string. This can be helpful when working with data that may have unwanted spaces, such as user input. For example: `SELECT TRIM(' Hello World ') AS trimmed_string;`. This query will return `'Hello World'` without the extra spaces at the beginning and end of the string.

23. **Working with Dates**: In addition to the basic `NOW()` and `DATE()` functions, MySQL offers more advanced date functions that allow you to manipulate date and time values. For example, the `DATE_ADD()` function allows you to add a specific interval (such as days, months, or years) to a date: `SELECT DATE_ADD('2025-01-01', INTERVAL 1 MONTH) AS new_date;`. This query will return `'2025-02-01'`, which is one month after the given date.

24. Similarly, the `DATE_SUB()` function allows you to subtract a specific interval from a date. For example, if you want to subtract 10 days from the current date, you could write: `SELECT DATE_SUB(NOW(), INTERVAL 10 DAY) AS new_date;`. This will return the date 10 days prior to the current date.

25. You can also use YEAR(), MONTH(), and DAY() functions to extract specific parts of a date. For example, to extract the year from a date, you would write: SELECT YEAR('2025-01-01') AS year_part;. This will return 2025. Similarly, you can use MONTH() and DAY() to extract the month and day parts of a date.

26. **Handling NULL Values**: In addition to IFNULL() and COALESCE(), MySQL offers several other functions for handling NULL values. For example, the NULLIF() function returns NULL if two expressions are equal, and the first expression otherwise. Here's an example: SELECT NULLIF(5, 5) AS result;. This will return NULL, as the two values are equal. If the values were different, the first value would be returned instead of NULL.

27. **Mathematical Functions Continued**: MySQL also provides more mathematical functions like MOD(), which returns the remainder of a division operation. For example: SELECT MOD(10, 3) AS remainder;. This query will return 1, as 10 divided by 3 leaves a remainder of 1.

28. The RAND() function returns a random floating-point number between 0 and 1. This can be useful when you need random values in your queries, such as when selecting a random row from a table. For example: SELECT RAND() AS random_value;. This will return a random number between 0 and 1, like 0.356457.

29. **Aggregate Functions Continued**: In addition to COUNT(), SUM(), AVG(), MIN(), and MAX(), MySQL offers some specialized aggregate functions. One such function is GROUP_CONCAT(), which concatenates the values of a column from multiple rows into a single string. This can be useful when you need to aggregate textual data. For example: SELECT customer_id, GROUP_CONCAT(order_id) AS order_ids FROM orders GROUP BY customer_id;. This query will return a concatenated list of all order IDs for each customer, allowing you to see all of a customer's orders in a single result.

30. Another useful aggregate function is STDDEV(), which calculates the standard deviation of a numeric column. For example: SELECT STDDEV(total_sales) AS sales_deviation FROM sales;. This query will return the standard deviation of the total_sales column, which helps measure the variation in sales.

31. **Subqueries and Functions**: In addition to using functions within basic queries, you can also use them in combination with subqueries for more complex operations. For example, to calculate the average sales for a product and then find all orders that exceed that average, you can use a subquery with the AVG() function: SELECT order_id, total_sales FROM orders WHERE total_sales > (SELECT AVG(total_sales) FROM sales WHERE product_id = 101);. This query uses a subquery to calculate the average sales for a specific product (with

product_id = 101) and then retrieves all orders where the total_sales exceed that average.

32. **String Matching Functions**: MySQL also provides several functions for pattern matching, which can be helpful when working with textual data. The LIKE operator is often used for basic pattern matching, but MySQL also provides more advanced functions like REGEXP for regular expression matching. For example: SELECT product_name FROM products WHERE product_name REGEXP '^A';. This query returns all products whose names begin with the letter "A". You can also use REGEXP to perform more complex pattern matching, such as matching a word or phrase within the text.

33. **User-defined Functions (UDFs)**: While MySQL comes with many built-in functions, you can also create your own **user-defined functions (UDFs)** to extend MySQL's functionality. UDFs allow you to define custom functions that can be used in your SQL queries. These functions are written in C or C++ and need to be compiled and installed on the MySQL server. Although UDFs are advanced and require server-level access to configure, they can be extremely useful for situations where built-in functions do not meet your needs.

34. **Best Practices for Using Functions**: When working with MySQL functions, there are several best practices to keep in mind:

- **Use Functions to Simplify Queries**: Functions can significantly simplify your queries by performing operations directly in SQL. Instead of processing data in your application code, you can leverage MySQL's built-in functions to perform tasks like date manipulation, string formatting, and mathematical calculations directly in your queries.

- **Consider Performance**: While functions are powerful, they can also add overhead to your queries. Functions like REGEXP or complex subqueries can slow down query performance, especially when dealing with large datasets. Always test and monitor your queries to ensure they are performing optimally.

- **Use Appropriate Functions**: Make sure to use the correct function for the task at hand. For example, use DATE_ADD() for date manipulation and ROUND() for rounding numbers, rather than attempting to perform these operations manually in your application logic.

35. **Conclusion**: MySQL functions are essential tools for manipulating and working with data directly in your SQL queries. From string manipulation to mathematical calculations and date handling, MySQL provides a wide range of functions to make your queries more efficient and powerful. In this chapter, we've covered basic string, numeric, date, and aggregate functions, along with best practices for using them. By mastering these functions, you'll be able to perform complex data transformations and optimizations directly within your queries. In the next chapter, we will explore **advanced query optimization techniques**, including how to fine-tune your MySQL queries for maximum

performance. Keep practicing with these functions, and you'll soon become proficient at writing efficient and effective MySQL queries!

Chapter 13: Data Integrity: Keys and Constraints

1. In this chapter, we will explore the concept of **data integrity** in MySQL and how it is enforced using **keys** and **constraints**. Data integrity ensures the accuracy, consistency, and reliability of data stored in the database. One of the key ways to enforce data integrity in MySQL is through the use of **primary keys**, **foreign keys**, **unique constraints**, and **other types of constraints**. By the end of this chapter, you will have a solid understanding of how keys and constraints work in MySQL and how they help maintain the quality of your data.

2. **Keys** are fundamental in maintaining data integrity, and they are used to define relationships between tables, uniquely identify records, and enforce rules on data. The two most important types of keys in relational databases are **primary keys** and **foreign keys**. In addition to these, **unique keys** and **composite keys** are also frequently used in MySQL. Let's begin by discussing **primary keys**, which are one of the most essential components of data integrity.

3. A **primary key** is a unique identifier for each record in a table. It ensures that each row in the table can be uniquely identified, which prevents duplicate records. A table can have only one primary key, and the primary key column(s) must contain unique values. It is also common practice to make the primary key column(s) **NOT NULL**, ensuring that no record can have a missing value for its primary key. Here's an example of how to create a table with a primary key: `CREATE TABLE customers ( customer_id INT NOT NULL, name VARCHAR(100), email VARCHAR(100), PRIMARY KEY (customer_id) );`. In this example, the `customer_id` column is the primary key, and it must be unique and not `NULL`.

4. **Foreign keys** are used to establish a relationship between two tables, and they help ensure referential integrity between the data. A foreign key in one table points to a primary key in another table. This means that the foreign key column in one table must contain values that match a value in the referenced primary key column of the other table. Foreign keys ensure that data in one table is consistent with data in another table, preventing orphaned records or inconsistent references. For example, consider the following query to create a `orders` table with a foreign key referencing the `customers` table: `CREATE TABLE orders ( order_id INT NOT NULL, customer_id INT, order_date DATE, PRIMARY KEY (order_id), FOREIGN KEY (customer_id) REFERENCES customers(customer_id) );`. In this case, the `customer_id` column in the `orders` table is a foreign key that references the `customer_id` column in the `customers` table, ensuring that each order is associated with an existing customer.

5. The **UNIQUE** constraint ensures that all values in a column are distinct. While the primary key enforces uniqueness and not nullability, the unique constraint allows you to enforce uniqueness on columns that are not the primary key. For example, if you want to ensure that each email address in the `customers` table is unique, you can add a unique constraint to the `email` column: `CREATE TABLE customers ( customer_id INT NOT NULL, name VARCHAR(100), email VARCHAR(100) UNIQUE, PRIMARY KEY (customer_id) );`. This query ensures that no two customers can have the same email address, enforcing data integrity for the `email` column.

6. **Composite keys** are keys that consist of more than one column. A composite primary key is useful when no single column can uniquely identify a row, but a combination of columns can. For example, in a `student_courses` table that records which courses each student is enrolled in, a combination of `student_id` and `course_id` may be used as the primary key: `CREATE TABLE student_courses ( student_id INT, course_id INT, enrollment_date DATE, PRIMARY KEY (student_id, course_id) );`. Here, the composite primary key ensures that each student can only be enrolled in the same course once. This prevents duplicate records for a student-course pair.

7. **NOT NULL** is one of the simplest and most widely used constraints in MySQL. It ensures that a column cannot contain NULL values, which is essential for enforcing data completeness. For example, if you want to ensure that every customer has a name and email, you can add the `NOT NULL` constraint: `CREATE TABLE customers ( customer_id INT NOT NULL, name VARCHAR(100) NOT NULL, email VARCHAR(100) NOT NULL, PRIMARY KEY (customer_id) );`. This query ensures that no customer record can have a `NULL` value for the `name` or `email` columns.

8. **CHECK** constraints are used to limit the values that can be inserted into a column. They ensure that the data meets certain conditions before it can be added to the table. For example, if you want to ensure that the `age` column in a `users` table only contains values between 18 and 100, you could create a `CHECK` constraint: `CREATE TABLE users ( user_id INT NOT NULL, name VARCHAR(100), age INT CHECK (age BETWEEN 18 AND 100), PRIMARY KEY (user_id) );`. This query ensures that only ages within the range of 18 to 100 can be inserted into the `age` column, enforcing data integrity and preventing invalid data.

9. **DEFAULT** constraints are used to assign a default value to a column if no value is provided during an insert operation. This ensures that columns have a valid value, even if the user does not explicitly provide one. For example, if you want to set a default status of 'active' for new customers, you can use the `DEFAULT` constraint: `CREATE TABLE customers ( customer_id INT NOT NULL, name`

VARCHAR(100), status VARCHAR(20) DEFAULT 'active', PRIMARY KEY (customer_id));. Here, if no status is provided when inserting a new record, MySQL will automatically set the status column to 'active'.

10. **Foreign Key Constraints**: The foreign key constraint not only helps maintain referential integrity but also provides options for what should happen when the data in the referenced table changes. The ON DELETE and ON UPDATE options define what happens when a referenced record is deleted or updated. For example, if a customer record is deleted, you may want to delete all related orders, or you may prefer to set the customer_id to NULL in the orders table: CREATE TABLE orders (order_id INT NOT NULL, customer_id INT, order_date DATE, PRIMARY KEY (order_id), FOREIGN KEY (customer_id) REFERENCES customers(customer_id) ON DELETE CASCADE ON UPDATE SET NULL);. In this example, ON DELETE CASCADE ensures that when a customer is deleted, all related orders are also deleted. ON UPDATE SET NULL ensures that if a customer_id is updated in the customers table, the customer_id in the orders table is set to NULL.

11. **Handling Invalid Data**: While keys and constraints help enforce data integrity, sometimes data can still be invalid due to user input errors, software bugs, or external issues. In such cases, it's important to handle the errors gracefully. MySQL provides the INSERT IGNORE, UPDATE IGNORE, and DELETE IGNORE statements, which ignore errors generated by constraint violations, allowing the query to continue without failing. For example, if you try to insert a record with a duplicate primary key but want to ignore the error, you can write: INSERT IGNORE INTO customers (customer_id, name, email) VALUES (101, 'John Doe', 'john.doe@example.com');. This statement ensures that if a customer with customer_id = 101 already exists, the insertion is ignored and no error is thrown.

12. **Enforcing Data Integrity at the Application Level**: While MySQL's keys and constraints provide the foundation for data integrity, it's also important to enforce integrity at the **application level**. This means performing validation checks in your application code before sending data to the database. For instance, you can check that a user's email address follows the correct format or that a product's price is non-negative before inserting it into the database. Combining database constraints with application-level validation provides an added layer of data integrity.

13. **Best Practices for Keys and Constraints**:

- Always define a **primary key** for every table to ensure each row is uniquely identifiable.
- Use **foreign keys** to enforce relationships between tables and maintain referential integrity.

- Avoid excessive use of **composite keys** unless necessary, as they can make queries and indexing more complex.
- Use **unique constraints** to ensure that columns like email addresses or usernames do not contain duplicate values.
- Apply **NOT NULL** constraints on columns that should never contain missing data (e.g., `email`, `username`).
- Regularly review your **foreign key relationships** to ensure that the `ON DELETE` and `ON UPDATE` actions are set correctly for your application's needs.

14. **Conclusion**: Keys and constraints are essential for ensuring data integrity in MySQL. By defining primary keys, foreign keys, unique constraints, and other constraints, you can enforce consistency, accuracy, and reliability in your data. In this chapter, we have covered the most common types of keys and constraints, including how to create them and how they work together to maintain data integrity. By using these tools properly, you can prevent invalid data, maintain relationships between tables, and ensure that your database operations are consistent and reliable. In the next chapter, we will explore **transactions and how to manage data consistency** in multi-step operations. Keep practicing with keys and constraints, and you'll soon become proficient in maintaining data integrity in MySQL!

15. **Handling Referential Integrity Violations**: When working with foreign keys, it's crucial to handle **referential integrity violations** properly. A referential integrity violation occurs when a foreign key in one table refers to a primary key in another table that no longer exists, such as when the referenced row in the parent table is deleted or updated in a way that no longer matches the foreign key value. To manage these violations, MySQL provides different strategies for the `ON DELETE` and `ON UPDATE` actions, such as `CASCADE`, `SET NULL`, and `NO ACTION`.

- **CASCADE**: When a referenced row is deleted or updated, the corresponding rows in the child table will be automatically deleted or updated. This is useful for maintaining consistency between the parent and child tables. Example: If a `customer` record is deleted, all their `order` records are also deleted.
  sql
  Copy

```
CREATE TABLE orders (
```

- ```
  order_id INT NOT NULL,
  ```
- ```
  customer_id INT,
  ```
- ```
  order_date DATE,
  ```
- ```
  PRIMARY KEY (order_id),
  ```

- FOREIGN KEY (customer_id) REFERENCES customers(customer_id)
- ON DELETE CASCADE
-);
-

- **SET NULL**: When a referenced row is deleted or updated, the foreign key in the child table is set to NULL. This ensures that the row is no longer tied to a non-existent row in the parent table. Example: If a `customer` is deleted, the `customer_id` in the `orders` table will be set to NULL for any related orders.
  sql
  Copy

  CREATE TABLE orders (

- order_id INT NOT NULL,
- customer_id INT,
- order_date DATE,
- PRIMARY KEY (order_id),
- FOREIGN KEY (customer_id) REFERENCES customers(customer_id)
- ON DELETE SET NULL
-);
-

- **NO ACTION**: If a referenced row is deleted or updated, MySQL will not take any action, and it will return an error if it violates the foreign key constraint. Example: If a `customer` is deleted, MySQL will prevent the deletion if there are any existing orders that refer to that customer.
  sql
  Copy

  CREATE TABLE orders (

- order_id INT NOT NULL,
- customer_id INT,
- order_date DATE,

- PRIMARY KEY (order_id),
- FOREIGN KEY (customer_id) REFERENCES customers(customer_id)
- ON DELETE NO ACTION
-);
-

16. **Handling Multiple Constraints on a Column**: In some cases, a single column may need to adhere to multiple constraints. For example, a column might need to be both `NOT NULL` and `UNIQUE`. MySQL allows you to define multiple constraints on a single column. For instance, in a `users` table where every email address must be both unique and non-null, you can combine these constraints:

sql
Copy
```
CREATE TABLE users (
  user_id INT NOT NULL AUTO_INCREMENT,
  email VARCHAR(100) NOT NULL UNIQUE,
  PRIMARY KEY (user_id)
);
```
Here, the `email` column is restricted to having non-null and unique values. This ensures that no user can have a `NULL` or duplicate email address in the table.

17. **Error Handling with Constraints**: It's important to handle errors effectively when working with constraints. When inserting, updating, or deleting data, MySQL will raise an error if the data violates any constraints. For instance, if you try to insert a duplicate value into a column with a `UNIQUE` constraint, MySQL will return an error. To handle such errors, you can use error handling mechanisms like `INSERT IGNORE` or `UPDATE IGNORE`, which allow the query to proceed without failing in case of constraint violations. For example:

sql
Copy
```
INSERT IGNORE INTO customers (customer_id, email) VALUES
(1, 'john.doe@example.com');
```
This will insert the data, but if the email already exists, the query will be ignored instead of throwing an error.

18. **Deferred Constraints**: In MySQL, constraints are generally enforced immediately after each SQL statement is executed. However, you can defer the checking of some constraints, such as foreign key constraints, until the end of a transaction. This can be useful in situations where you need to perform a series of operations that involve multiple

updates to related tables. MySQL does not support deferred constraints natively like some other relational databases (such as PostgreSQL), but you can simulate deferred constraints by using **transactions**. By wrapping your inserts, updates, or deletes in a transaction, you ensure that changes are only committed if all constraints are satisfied at the end of the transaction. Example:

sql
Copy
```
START TRANSACTION;

-- Update customer data
UPDATE customers SET status = 'inactive' WHERE customer_id
= 1;

-- Update orders linked to the customer
UPDATE orders SET status = 'cancelled' WHERE customer_id =
1;

COMMIT;
```

19. **Checking Integrity with the `SHOW TABLE STATUS` Command**: To check if the integrity constraints are properly set up and functioning as expected, you can use the `SHOW TABLE STATUS` command in MySQL. This command provides information about the tables in a database, including the number of rows, index size, and other relevant information. For example, to check the status of the `customers` table, you would write:

sql
Copy
```
SHOW TABLE STATUS LIKE 'customers';
```
This will provide details such as the table's engine, row format, number of rows, and data length, helping you to monitor the health of your tables and indexes.

20. **Best Practices for Keys and Constraints**:

- **Always define a primary key**: Every table should have a primary key to uniquely identify each record. This is the foundation of data integrity.
- **Use foreign keys to enforce relationships**: Foreign keys ensure that the data in related tables remains consistent. Always use them when dealing with related data.
- **Use appropriate constraints**: `NOT NULL`, `UNIQUE`, and `CHECK` constraints help ensure that your data meets the expected quality standards.

- **Balance performance and integrity**: While constraints help maintain data quality, they can also impact performance, particularly in write-heavy applications. Be selective about which constraints to apply based on your needs.

- **Avoid redundant indexes**: Ensure that indexes support the constraints you've defined, and avoid creating unnecessary or duplicate indexes, which can negatively impact performance.

21. **Troubleshooting Constraint Violations**: When constraints are violated, MySQL will return an error message indicating which constraint was violated. Common issues include trying to insert a duplicate value in a column with a `UNIQUE` constraint, inserting a `NULL` value into a column defined as `NOT NULL`, or attempting to delete a row that is referenced by a foreign key in another table. To troubleshoot constraint violations, examine the error message carefully, check the data that caused the violation, and verify that the appropriate constraints are applied to the relevant columns.

22. **Handling Constraints with Application Logic**: While MySQL constraints help maintain data integrity, it's also important to handle some aspects of data validation and integrity at the **application level**. For example, ensuring that user input is valid and sanitized before it's inserted into the database can help prevent constraint violations. Implementing input validation and proper error handling in your application ensures that the data entering your database is clean and accurate, reducing the risk of integrity issues.

23. **Conclusion**: Keys and constraints are essential tools for maintaining data integrity in MySQL. By enforcing rules such as uniqueness, referential integrity, and nullability, you can ensure that your data is accurate, consistent, and reliable. In this chapter, we have covered the most common types of keys and constraints, including primary keys, foreign keys, unique constraints, and check constraints, and discussed how to use them to enforce data quality in your MySQL databases. By properly utilizing keys and constraints, you will prevent invalid data from being entered into your tables and create a solid foundation for your database. In the next chapter, we will explore **transactions**, **locking**, and **rollback** operations, which will help you manage multi-step data operations and ensure data consistency in concurrent environments. Keep practicing with keys and constraints, and you'll soon be proficient in maintaining strong data integrity in MySQL!

Chapter 14: Managing Users and Permissions in MySQL

1. In this chapter, we will delve into the topic of **user management** and **permissions** in MySQL, which are essential for securing your database and ensuring that only authorized individuals can access and modify your data. MySQL provides a robust system for managing users and controlling their access to different parts of the database. This system helps ensure that sensitive data is protected while allowing users to perform necessary operations based on their roles. By the end of this chapter, you will have a solid understanding of how to create users, assign permissions, and manage access control in MySQL.

2. **User management** is a critical component of any relational database management system (RDBMS). MySQL uses a system of **user accounts** to manage access to the database. Each user account is associated with specific privileges, determining what the user can or cannot do. These privileges include the ability to read, write, update, delete, and administer the database. User accounts are created with the `CREATE USER` statement, which allows you to define a username and, optionally, a host from which the user can connect.

3. To create a new user in MySQL, you can use the `CREATE USER` command. The basic syntax is:

sql
Copy

```
CREATE USER 'username'@'host' IDENTIFIED BY 'password';
```

4.

For example, to create a user named `johndoe` who can connect from the local machine (`localhost`), you would write:

sql
Copy

```
CREATE USER 'johndoe'@'localhost' IDENTIFIED BY
'securepassword';
```

5.

This creates a user `johndoe` with the password `securepassword`, and they are restricted to logging in only from `localhost` (the local machine). If you want the user to connect from any host, you can use `'%'` as the host:

sql
Copy

```
CREATE USER 'johndoe'@'%' IDENTIFIED BY
'securepassword';
```

6.

7. **Granting Permissions**: Once a user is created, you need to grant them permissions to perform actions on the database. Permissions in MySQL are granted using the `GRANT` statement. The basic syntax for granting permissions is:
sql
Copy

```
GRANT permission_type ON database_name.table_name TO
'username'@'host';
```

8.

For example, to grant the `SELECT` permission (read-only access) on the `employees` table in the `company` database to the `johndoe` user, you would write:
sql
Copy

```
GRANT SELECT ON company.employees TO
'johndoe'@'localhost';
```

9.

This allows `johndoe` to read data from the `employees` table but not modify it. The `GRANT` statement can be used to grant a wide range of permissions, such as `INSERT`, `UPDATE`, `DELETE`, and even administrative privileges like `CREATE`, `DROP`, and `ALTER`.

10. **Global vs. Database-Level Permissions**: Permissions can be granted at various levels of granularity, including **global**, **database**, **table**, and **column** levels. A **global permission** applies to all databases in the MySQL server, while a **database-level permission** applies only to a specific database. For example:

    - To grant global `SELECT` permissions across all databases, you would use:
      sql
      Copy

      ```
      GRANT SELECT ON *.* TO 'johndoe'@'localhost';
      ```

o

o To grant SELECT permissions on a specific database (company), you would use:
sql
Copy

```sql
GRANT SELECT ON company.* TO
'johndoe'@'localhost';
```

o

11. **Administering Privileges**: In addition to granting permissions, MySQL also provides several administrative privileges that allow users to manage other users and permissions. These administrative privileges include:

    o **GRANT OPTION**: Allows a user to grant their own privileges to other users.

    o **CREATE USER**: Allows a user to create new user accounts.

    o **DROP USER**: Allows a user to drop (delete) user accounts.

    o **SHOW DATABASES**: Allows a user to see all databases on the MySQL server.

12. For example, to grant a user the ability to create and manage other users, you would grant the CREATE USER and GRANT OPTION privileges:
sql
Copy

```sql
GRANT CREATE USER, GRANT OPTION ON *.* TO
'adminuser'@'localhost';
```

13.

14. **Revoking Permissions**: If you need to revoke a user's privileges, you can use the REVOKE statement. This allows you to remove previously granted permissions. The syntax is similar to the GRANT statement:
sql

Copy

```
REVOKE permission_type ON database_name.table_name FROM
'username'@'host';
```

15.

For example, to revoke the `SELECT` permission on the `employees` table from the `johndoe` user, you would write:

sql
Copy

```
REVOKE SELECT ON company.employees FROM
'johndoe'@'localhost';
```

16.

This command removes the read-only access that was granted to `johndoe` on the `employees` table.

17. **Flushing Privileges**: After creating users or modifying their permissions, you need to reload the MySQL privilege tables to ensure the changes take effect. This can be done with the `FLUSH PRIVILEGES` statement:

sql
Copy

```
FLUSH PRIVILEGES;
```

18.

This command forces MySQL to reload the permission settings, ensuring that any changes made using the `GRANT` or `REVOKE` statements are immediately applied.

19. **Viewing User Privileges**: To check the permissions that have been granted to a particular user, you can use the `SHOW GRANTS` statement. For example:

sql
Copy

```
SHOW GRANTS FOR 'johndoe'@'localhost';
```

20\.

This command will display all of the permissions granted to the `johndoe` user, allowing you to review their access rights. You can use this to confirm what permissions have been granted or troubleshoot any access issues.

21\. **Using Roles for Permissions Management**: In MySQL 8.0 and later, you can use **roles** to manage permissions more efficiently. A role is a collection of permissions that can be granted to a user or other roles. This allows you to group related permissions and assign them collectively to multiple users. For example:

- First, create a role with a set of permissions:
  sql
  Copy

  ```
  CREATE ROLE 'read_only';
  ```

- `GRANT SELECT ON company.* TO 'read_only';`
-

- Then, assign the role to a user:
  sql
  Copy

  ```
  GRANT 'read_only' TO 'johndoe'@'localhost';
  ```

-

- If you want to revoke a role from a user:
  sql
  Copy

  ```
  REVOKE 'read_only' FROM 'johndoe'@'localhost';
  ```

o

22. **Temporary Users and Permissions**: Sometimes, you may need to create temporary users with limited permissions. This can be useful in situations where you want to provide access for a short period, such as during maintenance or troubleshooting. You can create a temporary user and grant them specific privileges, knowing that you can easily revoke access once their task is completed. Example:
sql
Copy

```
CREATE USER 'tempuser'@'localhost' IDENTIFIED BY
'temporarypassword';
```

23. `GRANT SELECT ON company.* TO 'tempuser'@'localhost';`
24. `-- Revoke access after the task is completed`
25. `REVOKE SELECT ON company.* FROM 'tempuser'@'localhost';`
26. `DROP USER 'tempuser'@'localhost';`
27.

28. **Best Practices for User Management**:

    - **Principle of Least Privilege**: Always grant users the minimum permissions required for them to perform their tasks. This reduces the risk of accidental or intentional data modification.
    - **Use Strong Passwords**: Ensure that user accounts use strong passwords to prevent unauthorized access.
    - **Regularly Review Permissions**: Periodically review user accounts and their permissions to ensure that they are still required and that no unnecessary privileges are granted.
    - **Use Roles for Ease of Management**: When managing large numbers of users, roles can simplify the process of granting and revoking permissions by grouping permissions together.

29. **Conclusion**: Managing users and permissions is a critical aspect of database security and integrity. In this chapter, we've learned how to create and manage users, grant and revoke permissions, and ensure that only authorized users have access to your database. By implementing user management practices like the principle of least privilege and using roles for easier permission management, you can maintain a secure and organized database environment. In the next chapter, we will explore **transactions and how to**

ensure data consistency across multiple operations. Keep practicing user management, and you'll soon be proficient in maintaining secure access controls in MySQL!

24. **Managing Access Control with Hosts**: MySQL allows you to define which host or IP address a user can connect from. This adds an additional layer of security by limiting user access to specific network locations. By default, when you create a user, they are allowed to connect only from the host you specify (such as `localhost`), but you can also allow access from any host (`%`) or from specific IP addresses or ranges.

For example, to allow a user to connect from any host, you would create the user as follows:

sql
Copy

```
CREATE USER 'johndoe'@'%' IDENTIFIED BY 'password';
```

Alternatively, you can restrict the user to a specific host or subnet:

sql
Copy

```
CREATE USER 'johndoe'@'192.168.1.10' IDENTIFIED BY
'password';  -- Specific IP address
CREATE USER 'johndoe'@'192.168.1.%' IDENTIFIED BY
'password';  -- IP range
```

This helps prevent unauthorized access to the MySQL server from unknown or unauthorized network locations.

25. **Password Management**: Securing user passwords is critical to protecting your MySQL database. MySQL provides several ways to handle password security, including enforcing strong password policies and changing passwords.

- **Setting a Password**: You can set or change a user's password using the `ALTER USER` command. For example, to change the password for `johndoe`, you would write:
  sql
  Copy

  ```
  ALTER USER 'johndoe'@'localhost' IDENTIFIED BY
  'newpassword';
  ```

-

- **Password Expiry**: To enhance security, you can set an expiration date for a user's password, forcing them to change it after a specified period. To set a password expiration, you can use:

sql
Copy

```
ALTER USER 'johndoe'@'localhost' PASSWORD EXPIRE
INTERVAL 90 DAY;
```

-

This query forces the user to change their password every 90 days.

- **Password Strength Policies**: MySQL supports the `validate_password` plugin, which helps enforce password strength rules. You can configure it to require passwords to have a minimum length, include a mix of characters, and contain numeric and special characters. For example, to enable this plugin and set the minimum password length to 8 characters:
  sql
  Copy

```
INSTALL PLUGIN validate_password SONAME
'validate_password.so';
```

- `SET GLOBAL validate_password.policy = STRONG;`
- `SET GLOBAL validate_password.length = 8;`
-

16. **Revoking Permissions**: The REVOKE statement removes specific permissions from a user. This is useful when a user no longer requires access to a particular resource or if their role changes. For instance, to revoke the UPDATE permission on the `orders` table for the user `johndoe`, you would write:

sql
Copy

```
REVOKE UPDATE ON orders FROM 'johndoe'@'localhost';
```

The REVOKE statement can also be used to remove global or database-level permissions. After revoking permissions, it is important to use the `FLUSH PRIVILEGES` command to apply the changes:

sql
Copy

```
FLUSH PRIVILEGES;
```

17. **Removing a User**: If a user no longer needs access to the MySQL server, you can remove their account entirely using the `DROP USER` command. This will delete the user and all their associated privileges. For example, to delete the `johndoe` user:

sql
Copy
```
DROP USER 'johndoe'@'localhost';
```
Be cautious when dropping users, especially if they have many privileges or if there are active connections. You can check for any active connections using the `SHOW PROCESSLIST` command and terminate them before dropping the user.

18. **Audit Logging and Monitoring**: Monitoring user activities is an important aspect of managing security. MySQL offers the **Audit Plugin** to help track user actions, such as successful and failed login attempts, executed queries, and any modifications made to the database.

You can install the MySQL Enterprise Audit plugin to log specific queries and track activities. The audit logs can be analyzed to detect unusual patterns of access or potential security breaches. For example, you can track login attempts, query executions, or changes to user accounts, which can help maintain security and comply with data protection regulations.

- To install and configure the MySQL Enterprise Audit plugin, you would use the following commands:
  sql
  Copy

  ```
  INSTALL PLUGIN audit_log SONAME 'audit_log.so';
  ```
- ```
  SET GLOBAL audit_log_policy = 'LOGINS';
  ```
-

19. **Using the `SHOW GRANTS` Command**: It's a good practice to regularly check the privileges granted to users. You can use the `SHOW GRANTS` statement to view the permissions assigned to a specific user:

sql
Copy
```
SHOW GRANTS FOR 'johndoe'@'localhost';
```
This will display a list of all the permissions the user has, allowing you to verify that they only have the necessary access.
```

20. **Granting and Revoking Permissions on Tables, Columns, and Views**: MySQL allows you to be very granular with your permissions by assigning them not only to databases but also to individual tables, columns, and views. For example, to grant the `SELECT` permission on a specific column of a table, you can use the following:

sql
Copy
```
GRANT SELECT (column_name) ON database_name.table_name TO
'johndoe'@'localhost';
```
Similarly, you can revoke permissions on specific tables or columns:

sql
Copy
```
REVOKE SELECT (column_name) ON database_name.table_name
FROM 'johndoe'@'localhost';
```
21. **Backup and Recovery of User Accounts**: It's important to back up your MySQL user accounts and their privileges. MySQL provides the ability to export user privileges using the `mysqldump` utility. The following command creates a backup of the MySQL system database, which includes user accounts and privileges:

bash
Copy
```
mysqldump -u root -p --all-databases --routines --triggers
--flush-logs --events > mysql_backup.sql
```
This ensures that user accounts and their corresponding permissions can be restored in case of an emergency or system failure.

22. **Best Practices for User and Permission Management**:

- **Use the Principle of Least Privilege**: Always grant the minimum permissions necessary for a user to perform their job functions. Avoid giving broad privileges unless absolutely necessary.

- **Regularly Review User Accounts and Permissions**: Periodically review user access and revoke permissions that are no longer required. This will help minimize the potential for unauthorized access.

- **Use Strong Authentication and Password Policies**: Enforce strong password policies to prevent weak or easily guessable passwords. Consider using multi-factor authentication (MFA) for added security.

- **Limit Remote Access**: Restrict user access to MySQL to only those who require it and limit access to specific IP addresses or hosts.

- **Use Roles for Simpler Permissions Management**: When managing large numbers of users, consider using roles to group permissions and simplify the process of granting and revoking access.

23. **Troubleshooting Permissions Issues**: One of the most common issues when managing MySQL users is ensuring that the user has the correct permissions to perform a specific action. If a user encounters an error when trying to access data, use the following steps to troubleshoot:

- Verify the user's privileges using the `SHOW GRANTS` command.
- Check if the user is connecting from the correct host and whether the host is allowed in the user account configuration.
- Ensure that the required database, table, or column permissions are granted.
- Use the `EXPLAIN` statement for complex queries to see if the user has sufficient privileges to execute them.

24. **Conclusion**: Managing users and permissions in MySQL is critical for securing your database and ensuring that data is accessed and modified only by authorized individuals. In this chapter, we have covered the basics of user management, including how to create users, grant and revoke permissions, and manage access control at various levels. We've also discussed best practices for securing user accounts, troubleshooting permission issues, and using roles for more efficient permission management. By mastering user and permission management, you will be able to ensure the security and integrity of your MySQL databases. In the next chapter, we will explore **transactions and how to maintain data consistency** in multi-step operations. Keep practicing user management, and you'll soon be proficient in securing and maintaining access to your MySQL databases!

Chapter 15: MySQL Transactions: Ensuring Consistency

1. In this chapter, we will explore **transactions** in MySQL and how they help ensure data consistency and integrity, especially in complex operations involving multiple queries. A transaction is a sequence of one or more SQL operations executed as a single unit. If all the operations in a transaction are successful, the changes are committed to the database; if any operation fails, the entire transaction is rolled back, leaving the database in a consistent state. By the end of this chapter, you will understand how to use transactions in MySQL to maintain data consistency and integrity, even in the face of errors or failures.

2. **What Is a Transaction?** A transaction is a sequence of operations that are treated as a single unit. Transactions allow you to group multiple queries together, ensuring that either all the queries succeed or none of them are applied. This is particularly useful when performing operations that require multiple steps, such as transferring money between two bank accounts or updating multiple tables in a database. Transactions in MySQL are based on the **ACID** properties: **Atomicity**, **Consistency**, **Isolation**, and **Durability**.

- **Atomicity**: A transaction is atomic, meaning that all the operations in the transaction are completed successfully, or none of them are applied. If one operation fails, the entire transaction is rolled back.
- **Consistency**: The transaction ensures that the database moves from one consistent state to another. If the transaction is successful, the database remains in a valid state.
- **Isolation**: Transactions are isolated from each other, meaning that the operations of one transaction are not visible to other transactions until they are committed.
- **Durability**: Once a transaction is committed, its changes are permanent and will survive system failures.

3. **Starting a Transaction**: In MySQL, a transaction begins with the `START TRANSACTION` or `BEGIN` command. This indicates that the following operations are part of a transaction and should not be committed until the `COMMIT` statement is issued. For example:

sql
Copy

```
START TRANSACTION;
```

4.

This begins a transaction, and all subsequent queries will be part of this transaction until it is either committed or rolled back.

5. **Committing a Transaction**: Once all the operations in a transaction are completed successfully, you can use the `COMMIT` statement to save the changes to the database. This makes the changes permanent and visible to other transactions. For example:

sql
Copy

```
COMMIT;
```

6.

This command commits all changes made during the transaction to the database, ensuring that they are permanently stored.

7. **Rolling Back a Transaction**: If an error occurs during the transaction or if you decide to cancel the transaction, you can use the `ROLLBACK` statement to undo all changes made during the transaction. This restores the database to its state before the transaction began, ensuring consistency. For example:

sql

Copy

```
ROLLBACK;
```

8.

This command will undo all changes made in the current transaction, rolling back any updates, inserts, or deletes performed during the transaction.

9. **Using Transactions for Complex Operations**: Transactions are particularly useful when performing operations that involve multiple steps. For example, suppose you are transferring money from one bank account to another, which involves two operations: deducting money from one account and adding it to another. To ensure that either both operations succeed or neither are applied, you can use a transaction:

sql

Copy

```
START TRANSACTION;
```

10.
11. `UPDATE accounts SET balance = balance - 100 WHERE account_id = 1;  -- Deduct money from account 1`
12. `UPDATE accounts SET balance = balance + 100 WHERE account_id = 2;  -- Add money to account 2`
13.
14. `COMMIT;`
15.

If any of the `UPDATE` operations fail, you can roll back the entire transaction to ensure that the money is not deducted from one account without being added to the other.

16. **Transaction Isolation Levels**: MySQL supports different **isolation levels** to control how transactions interact with each other. The isolation level defines the degree to which one transaction's operations are isolated from the operations of other concurrent transactions. The four main isolation levels in MySQL are:

- **READ UNCOMMITTED**: Allows transactions to read data that has been modified by other transactions but not yet committed. This level provides the least isolation but the highest concurrency.
- **READ COMMITTED**: Allows transactions to read only committed data. This prevents dirty reads (reading uncommitted data), but non-repeatable reads (where the data changes between reads) may still occur.
- **REPEATABLE READ**: Ensures that if a transaction reads a value, it will see the same value if it reads it again within the same transaction. This level prevents both dirty reads and non-repeatable reads but still allows phantom reads (where new rows are inserted that match the transaction's query).
- **SERIALIZABLE**: The highest isolation level, which ensures that transactions are executed in such a way that they appear to be executed one at a time, serially. This level prevents dirty reads, non-repeatable reads, and phantom reads but can lead to lower concurrency.

17. You can set the isolation level for a transaction using the `SET TRANSACTION` command:
 sql
 Copy

```
SET TRANSACTION ISOLATION LEVEL READ COMMITTED;
```

18.

19. **Deadlocks and Handling Deadlocks**: A **deadlock** occurs when two or more transactions are waiting for each other to release locks on resources, causing them to be stuck in a cycle. MySQL automatically detects deadlocks and rolls back one of the transactions to break the cycle, allowing the other transactions to proceed.
 To handle deadlocks effectively, make sure to:
 - Keep transactions short and efficient.
 - Access tables and rows in the same order across different transactions.
 - Use the `InnoDB` storage engine, which supports row-level locking and better deadlock detection.

20. You can check for deadlocks by examining the MySQL error log or using the `SHOW ENGINE INNODB STATUS` command:
 sql

Copy

```
SHOW ENGINE INNODB STATUS;
```

21.

22. **Savepoints in Transactions**: MySQL supports **savepoints**, which allow you to create intermediate points within a transaction. If an error occurs, you can roll back to a specific savepoint rather than rolling back the entire transaction. This provides finer control over which operations to undo. For example:
    sql
    Copy

```
START TRANSACTION;
```

23.
24. `SAVEPOINT point1;`
25. `UPDATE accounts SET balance = balance - 100 WHERE account_id = 1;   -- Deduct money from account 1`
26.
27. `SAVEPOINT point2;`
28. `UPDATE accounts SET balance = balance + 100 WHERE account_id = 2;   -- Add money to account 2`
29.
30. `-- Roll back to point2 if there's an error`
31. `ROLLBACK TO SAVEPOINT point2;`
32.
33. `COMMIT;`
34.

    In this example, if an error occurs during the second `UPDATE` statement, the transaction can be rolled back to `point2`, leaving the first `UPDATE` operation intact.

35. **Transactional Data Integrity**: Transactions help ensure **data consistency** by preventing partial updates that could leave the database in an inconsistent state. By using transactions, MySQL ensures that the database remains in a valid state even in the case of system crashes or application failures. For example, in a bank transfer scenario, if a failure occurs after money is deducted from one account but before it is added to another,

a transaction ensures that no partial changes are made. Using transactions guarantees that either both operations succeed or neither do.

36. **Nested Transactions**: While MySQL does not support true **nested transactions**, you can simulate them using **savepoints**. As mentioned earlier, you can create savepoints within a transaction and roll back to specific points without affecting the entire transaction. This allows you to handle sub-operations more efficiently within a larger transaction.

37. **Transaction Performance Considerations**: While transactions help ensure data consistency, they can impact performance, particularly in write-heavy applications. Long-running transactions can hold locks on tables and rows, preventing other transactions from accessing the same data and leading to performance bottlenecks. To optimize transaction performance:

    - Keep transactions as short as possible.
    - Avoid long waits for user input or network delays during transactions.
    - Use appropriate indexes to reduce the time required to locate and modify rows.
    - Consider using batch operations to reduce the number of transactions.

38. **Best Practices for Using Transactions**:

    - **Start and commit transactions as quickly as possible**: Begin a transaction only when necessary, and commit or roll back as soon as possible to minimize locking and improve concurrency.
    - **Use appropriate isolation levels**: Set the correct isolation level based on your application's requirements for consistency and concurrency.
    - **Handle deadlocks gracefully**: Design your application to detect and handle deadlocks, either by retrying the transaction or by notifying the user if necessary.
    - **Test transactions thoroughly**: Test complex transaction scenarios to ensure that all operations work as expected, especially when rolling back or handling failures.

39. **Conclusion**: Transactions are a powerful tool in MySQL for ensuring data consistency, integrity, and reliability. By grouping multiple operations together and applying the principles of **ACID**, transactions help maintain the integrity of your database, even in the face of errors or failures. In this chapter, we've covered how to use transactions in MySQL, including starting, committing, and rolling back transactions, as well as managing isolation levels and deadlocks. By following best practices and optimizing your transaction management, you can ensure that your applications maintain data integrity and perform efficiently. In the next chapter, we will explore **locking mechanisms in MySQL**, which are crucial for managing concurrency and preventing issues in multi-user environments. Keep practicing with transactions, and you'll soon be able to manage complex data operations with confidence!

Chapter 16: Optimizing MySQL Queries for Better Performance

1. When it comes to working with MySQL, the phrase "speed matters" can often feel like the underappreciated sibling to "data integrity." But let's face it—nobody wants their database queries to take ages. It's like asking a taxi driver for a ride from New York to Los Angeles and expecting to get there in 10 minutes. So, why settle for a sluggish database when you could be working with a Ferrari? This chapter will walk you through optimizing your MySQL queries like a seasoned race car mechanic, with a few laughs along the way. Performance optimization isn't just about making things faster—it's about making smarter choices and keeping your queries lean and mean. And trust me, you want your queries to be lean, not the ones that come out of a "please-wait-for-forever" queue. Fast queries are happy queries, and happy queries make for happy developers.

2. The first step to any successful query optimization effort is understanding what's going on under the hood. In MySQL, the **query execution plan** is like your query's Google Maps—without it, you might be taking a detour straight into a dead-end of inefficiency. Enter `EXPLAIN`, a tool that offers a snapshot of how MySQL plans to execute your query. It tells you which indexes are used, how tables are joined, and whether you're about to do a full table scan (hint: it's not a good thing unless you're running a bakery and need to scan everything for an ingredient). By using `EXPLAIN`, you get a peek under the hood, which is far less messy than getting your hands greasy in your SQL engine. For example, try running `EXPLAIN SELECT * FROM products WHERE price > 100;`—and prepare for some insight into whether you've got an optimized query or a completely inefficient one.

3. Speaking of indexing, let's talk about **indexes**—your SQL engine's secret weapon for speedy retrieval. Imagine trying to find a book in a library, but instead of using the Dewey Decimal System, you just go down every aisle randomly, hoping to find what you need. That's a full table scan. Now, imagine using an index to go straight to the right shelf. That's how indexing works—well, without the paper cuts from turning the pages. When you create an index on columns that are frequently used in `WHERE` clauses or `JOIN` conditions, MySQL can quickly pinpoint the data you need, reducing query time significantly. So, if you're not using indexes, you're basically telling MySQL, "Take your time." And let's be real, nobody likes that guy.

4. But, like everything in life, **balance is key**. If you have too many indexes on a table, it's like trying to drive a car with all the windows down in a windstorm—sure, you're moving fast, but everything is getting blown around. Too many indexes can actually slow down `INSERT`, `UPDATE`, and `DELETE` operations because MySQL has to maintain the indexes every time a change is made. The trick is to create indexes on columns that are **frequently queried**, not just because you think "Hey, more indexes, more speed!" For example, indexing every column in your database is a bit like having every available condiment on your burger—looks impressive, but you'll be choking on it by the first bite.

5. Now, let's talk about **SELECT * FROM**—also known as the SQL equivalent of a free-for-all buffet. Sure, you can get all the data, but are you really sure you need it all? If

your query looks like it's asking for everything under the sun, it might be time to reconsider. Selecting all columns from a table might seem like a quick fix, but you're potentially dragging an entire banquet of unnecessary data across the network. Stick to selecting only the columns you need, and watch your queries slim down. It's like ordering the salad instead of the three-course meal—you're only taking what you can actually consume. For example, instead of `SELECT * FROM employees`, try `SELECT employee_id, first_name FROM employees;`. Short and sweet, right?

6. As you dig deeper into optimizing queries, it's important to consider how your data is **structured**. Not all tables are created equal, and sometimes a little restructuring is needed. For example, breaking down a massive table into smaller, more manageable **partitions** can improve performance significantly. Think of it like organizing your bookshelf—if every book is in one giant pile, it'll take you forever to find that one book on quantum mechanics. But if you divide the books into genres (or better yet, by Dewey Decimal), you'll be breezing through the library in no time. Partitioning a table by date or region, for example, helps MySQL focus on a smaller subset of data, cutting down on the time spent searching.

7. But wait, there's more! MySQL's **query cache** is like the magical fridge that keeps food fresh so you don't have to cook every time. Once a query has been executed, MySQL stores the result in memory. So, when the same query is run again, it can just pull out the results from the cache, instead of cooking up the same query again. However, this works best for **read-heavy** workloads, where data doesn't change frequently. If your query results are dynamic, using the query cache might not be as beneficial. Also, don't expect MySQL's query cache to work its magic on every query, especially those with complex joins or large result sets. So, while the query cache is helpful, don't rely on it like the pizza delivery guy—it doesn't always show up when you expect.

8. If your database is feeling a little sluggish, one thing you might want to try is optimizing **joins**. Joins are like the SQL equivalent of mixing ingredients together to make a delicious dish, but they can get messy if you're not careful. If you're joining large tables, ensure that the join columns are **indexed**. Without indexing, MySQL might end up searching through entire tables, which is like finding a needle in a haystack. Use the most restrictive join first—get the small set of data quickly, then move on to the larger one. And when you have the option, use `INNER JOIN` instead of `LEFT JOIN`. `INNER JOIN` is more efficient because it only returns rows that have matching data in both tables. Keep it lean.

9. Now, let's talk about **subqueries**—those sneaky little guys that often pop up in SQL queries. Subqueries can be powerful, but they sometimes leave you in the same situation as a rabbit stuck in a hole: going round and round. Subqueries that are correlated (those that refer back to the outer query) can particularly slow things down. Instead of nesting them, try using **joins** or **temporary tables** to simplify your query. A query with subqueries can quickly become a convoluted mess, like that time you tried to explain how your relationship with your dog is totally non-transactional.

10. **Aggregations** are another area where MySQL can get bogged down. Whether it's COUNT(), SUM(), or AVG(), aggregation functions often require MySQL to process large amounts of data. To optimize them, first make sure your data is indexed in a way that helps MySQL quickly access the rows needed for aggregation. The key here is to reduce the number of rows being processed before performing the aggregation. If you're summing sales data, for example, don't include all orders in the past decade—filter out old data with WHERE clauses so you're only aggregating what's relevant. Think of it like skipping the lettuce on your burger to get straight to the good stuff.

11. And speaking of aggregates, if you're performing **GROUP BY** operations, consider **indexing** the columns you're grouping by. If you're grouping by customer_id, ensure that customer_id is indexed. If MySQL can quickly access the necessary rows via the index, it can group them more efficiently. Without an index, MySQL may need to process every row before grouping them, like sorting through your entire wardrobe for a missing sock. So, go ahead and index those columns and let MySQL focus on the important stuff.

12. **Data types** matter more than you think. Selecting the right data type for your columns can save you both storage space and query time. For example, using INT instead of BIGINT when you don't need the larger range of numbers can save storage space and improve performance. Similarly, using VARCHAR(255) for a column that only stores short strings is a waste of space. Choose the smallest data type possible that will still accommodate your data, and you'll notice improvements in both speed and efficiency. It's like choosing the right-sized suitcase—you don't want it too big, or you'll be carrying around extra baggage.

13. **Temporary tables** are another great tool in your query optimization toolkit. If you have a complex query that's making multiple passes over the same data, consider using a **temporary table** to store intermediate results. Temporary tables allow you to break a complex query into smaller, more manageable parts, making it easier for MySQL to process. It's like taking the cake batter and putting it in separate bowls to mix instead of trying to make a giant cake in one go.

14. **Avoiding locking issues** is also key to performance optimization. If multiple transactions are constantly locking the same rows, your queries can become sluggish. To prevent this, try to keep transactions short, access rows in the same order, and make sure your queries are well-indexed. If you need to lock a table, use **LOCK TABLES** carefully, because unnecessary locks can slow down your entire system. It's like trying to cross a busy intersection with a line of pedestrians—don't cause unnecessary congestion.

15. **Limit the use of DISTINCT**: While DISTINCT is a useful tool when you need to eliminate duplicates from a result set, it can be slow when dealing with large datasets. If possible, try to eliminate duplicates earlier in the query or make use of indexes to reduce the data that needs to be processed. Remember, DISTINCT isn't your go-to fix for

poorly structured queries—it's more like a Band-Aid on a wound that needs proper treatment.

16. **Stored procedures** can be a game-changer when it comes to optimizing queries. If you have a complex query that runs frequently, consider turning it into a **stored procedure**. Stored procedures are precompiled, meaning they are executed more quickly than normal queries. Think of stored procedures like taking a shortcut through a back alley rather than walking down a crowded street—you get to your destination faster.

17. **Batching operations** is another optimization trick that helps when dealing with large datasets. Instead of running a single query that tries to update thousands of rows, break it up into smaller, more manageable batches. This allows MySQL to handle the load more efficiently and avoids locking too many rows at once. It's like lifting weights—better to do sets of 10 reps than try to lift the entire barbell at once.

18. **Avoid using functions on indexed columns**: If you use a function in the `WHERE` clause on an indexed column, MySQL may not use the index, forcing it to scan the entire table. For example, using `YEAR(order_date) = 2020` on an indexed `order_date` column can prevent MySQL from using the index. Instead, rewrite the query to avoid using the function, or try to restructure it so the indexed column is used directly.

19. **Optimizing joins with subqueries**: A common performance issue arises when a query requires multiple subqueries, each of which needs to be executed. Consider whether the subqueries can be replaced with a join, as joins tend to be more efficient. For example, rather than using a subquery to get the maximum value for each group, try to rewrite it as a join, which could reduce the number of queries MySQL needs to execute.

20. **Partitioning large tables**: If your table is extremely large and your queries frequently filter based on a specific column (like a date or region), consider partitioning the table. Partitioning splits the table into smaller, more manageable parts, allowing MySQL to focus on just the relevant partitions when running queries. It's like organizing your bookshelf by genre, instead of just having one big stack of books.

21. **Use of `HAVING` vs. `WHERE`**: The `HAVING` clause is often used after an aggregation, but it can be slower than `WHERE` when used incorrectly. Use `WHERE` for filtering rows before they are aggregated, and reserve `HAVING` for conditions that filter after the aggregation. Using `WHERE` can often prevent unnecessary aggregation, making your queries faster.

22. **Use `LIMIT` to reduce data size**: When you don't need to process the entire result set, use `LIMIT` to restrict the number of rows returned. For example, if you're developing an application that shows only the top 10 most recent orders, use `LIMIT 10` to ensure that MySQL only processes the necessary rows.

23. **Query profiling**: For large-scale applications or performance-critical queries, use **query profiling** to get detailed statistics on query execution times. Profiling allows you to identify the slowest parts of your queries and fine-tune them. For example:

sql
Copy
```
SET profiling = 1;
SELECT * FROM orders WHERE customer_id = 101;
SHOW PROFILES;
```

24. **Conclusion**: Optimizing MySQL queries is an ongoing process. By understanding the intricacies of MySQL's query execution plan, using indexes effectively, and applying best practices like batching operations and reducing function calls on indexed columns, you can make sure your queries stay fast and efficient. You don't have to settle for slow performance—apply these strategies, and you'll have your MySQL database running like a well-oiled machine. Happy querying, and may your queries always be speedy!

25. **Bonus Tip**: If all else fails, just reboot the server. It works surprisingly well for the problems you don't want to admit are happening. Just kidding. Sort of.

Chapter 17: Advanced Joins and Data Relationships

1. Welcome to the realm of **advanced joins and data relationships**, where MySQL transforms into an oracle of efficiency, and your queries—once slow and cumbersome—become sleek and agile. If you're not already comfortable with basic joins, like `INNER JOIN` or `LEFT JOIN`, well, let's just say it's time to graduate from driving a tricycle to handling a sports car. In this chapter, we'll dive deeper into the sophisticated world of SQL joins and relationships that will allow you to handle complex datasets like a pro. You're no longer a newbie in this SQL world, so let's break down the advanced techniques with a mix of practical tips and humor—because who said optimization can't be fun?

2. First, let's talk about the **self join**, which sounds like an existential crisis for your database, but don't worry, it's not as dramatic as it sounds. A self join occurs when you join a table with itself. Imagine you have a list of employees, and each employee has a `manager_id` that references another employee. To find out who reports to whom, you can perform a self join. It's like asking your database, "Who's your boss?" without needing to hire a private investigator. For example:

   sql
   Copy

   ```
   SELECT e.employee_name, m.employee_name AS manager_name
   ```

3. `FROM employees e`
4. `LEFT JOIN employees m ON e.manager_id = m.employee_id;`

5.

This query gives you a list of employees along with their managers, and it's as simple as asking your database for a family tree!

6. **Multiple joins** can make your queries more complex, but with great complexity comes great power (and sometimes slower queries, but we'll deal with that later). When joining more than two tables, make sure you're following the data flow like you're assembling a sandwich: layer by layer. You need to know the order of operations to avoid a SQL disaster. For instance, let's say you want to find customers, the products they ordered, and the employees who handled their orders. With multiple joins, this could look like:

sql

Copy

```
SELECT c.customer_name, p.product_name, e.employee_name
```

7. `FROM customers c`
8. `INNER JOIN orders o ON c.customer_id = o.customer_id`
9. `INNER JOIN products p ON o.product_id = p.product_id`
10. `INNER JOIN employees e ON o.employee_id = e.employee_id;`
11.

Each table is added with a reason, and the query flows smoothly, like a culinary masterpiece.

12. **Cross joins**, on the other hand, are like the wild card in the deck. They can be useful, but be careful—you don't want to create a mess. A cross join returns the Cartesian product of two tables, meaning every row from one table is paired with every row from the other. It's like ordering one of everything from a restaurant menu—looks tempting, but you may regret it later. For example, if you have a `colors` table with 3 rows and a `sizes` table with 4 rows, a cross join will return 12 rows (3 x 4):

sql

Copy

```
SELECT color, size
```

13. `FROM colors`
14. `CROSS JOIN sizes;`

15.

This might come in handy for generating combinations of data, but avoid it when your tables are large—otherwise, you'll be dealing with performance issues the way you deal with an overstuffed suitcase.

16. **Natural joins** may sound like a trend in the world of organic food, but in MySQL, they're a special type of join where the database automatically joins tables based on columns with the same name. While they save time and make queries look cleaner, they can be tricky. Like mixing too many ingredients in a pot, the results might not always be what you expect. When using natural joins, MySQL will assume that the matching column names mean you want to join on those columns. For example:

sql

Copy

```
SELECT e.employee_name, d.department_name
```

17. `FROM employees e`
18. `NATURAL JOIN departments d;`
19.

This works great when the column names match and you trust MySQL's intuition, but be careful if the tables have columns with the same name but different meanings.

20. **Using joins with aggregation** can turn your query into a finely tuned machine that extracts the most out of your data. Imagine you have a table of orders, and you want to know the total sales for each customer. Not only do you need to join the tables correctly, but you also need to aggregate the results to get a meaningful total. Here's how you'd do it:

sql

Copy

```
SELECT c.customer_name, SUM(o.order_total) AS
total_spent
```

21. `FROM customers c`
22. `INNER JOIN orders o ON c.customer_id = o.customer_id`
23. `GROUP BY c.customer_name;`
24.

This query groups the customers and sums their order totals. Aggregations and joins work together like a well-rehearsed dance, but without the missteps.

25. **Subqueries in joins** are like the chocolate chips in your query cookie. They might seem unnecessary at first, but they're the secret ingredient that can make everything come together. A subquery within a join can allow you to retrieve a specific subset of data and join it with another table. For example, if you wanted to find customers who spent more than the average order amount, you can use a subquery in a join:

    sql
    Copy

    ```
    SELECT c.customer_name, o.order_total
    ```

26. `FROM customers c`
27. `JOIN orders o ON c.customer_id = o.customer_id`
28. `WHERE o.order_total > (SELECT AVG(order_total) FROM orders);`
29.

    This query finds customers who spent more than the average order value, demonstrating that subqueries can provide nuanced insights when combined with joins.

30. **Left joins vs. right joins**—it's the battle of the directions, and much like deciding whether to go left or right on your morning jog, the choice of `LEFT JOIN` or `RIGHT JOIN` depends on your needs. The fundamental difference lies in which table you want to include all rows from when there's no match. With a `LEFT JOIN`, you get all rows from the left table and matching rows from the right table. With a `RIGHT JOIN`, you get all rows from the right table and matching rows from the left. Both are useful, but be mindful of which table holds the majority of your data. Sometimes, the answer to "left or right?" depends on whether you want to prioritize the "left" side's completeness or the "right" side's exclusivity.

31. **Join optimization** is like finding the best route on your GPS app—you want to minimize the time spent while avoiding unnecessary detours. When you're working with multiple joins, the order in which you join tables can have a huge impact on performance. For example, if you're joining five tables, MySQL will choose an optimal execution plan based on the size and structure of your data, but it's still a good idea to consider which tables are smaller or more selective. Start with the smaller tables in your joins and progressively build out the query. By reducing the number of rows early in the query, you're helping MySQL stay focused and speedy.

32. **Joins with conditions** can make your queries even more powerful. Sometimes you don't just want to join tables, you want to apply specific conditions to the join itself. This is where `ON` and `USING` clauses become your best friends. You can add conditions to your

join that act as filters, making the result set more relevant. For example:
sql
Copy

```
SELECT o.order_id, c.customer_name
```

33. `FROM orders o`
34. `JOIN customers c ON o.customer_id = c.customer_id AND o.order_date > '2023-01-01';`
35.

This query only returns orders that occurred after January 1, 2023, and ensures that the join condition is tightly coupled with the filtering logic.

36. **Composite joins** are like putting together the ultimate playlist—each element is better when combined. When you need to join on more than one column, you can use composite joins. This means joining tables based on multiple columns, often when a single column doesn't uniquely identify the relationship. For example, let's say we're joining two tables that require a combination of `first_name` and `last_name` to uniquely identify a relationship:
sql
Copy

```
SELECT e.first_name, e.last_name, d.department_name
```

37. `FROM employees e`
38. `JOIN departments d ON e.first_name = d.first_name AND e.last_name = d.last_name;`
39.

Composite joins ensure that MySQL matches records more precisely by combining multiple columns. It's like the perfect duo in a movie—nothing beats the power of two.

40. **Avoiding Cartesian products** is one of the classic mistakes when it comes to joins. Imagine trying to sort a thousand pages of a book by randomly shuffling the chapters—it's a mess. A Cartesian product occurs when you forget to specify the join condition, resulting in a query that combines every row of one table with every row of another. For example:
sql
Copy

```
SELECT * FROM orders, customers;
```

41.

This will return a massive set of rows, and in a large dataset, the results can quickly balloon to millions of records. To avoid this, always ensure that every join has a proper ON condition to prevent this unintentional chaos.

42. **Using self joins in hierarchical data** is one of the most effective ways to model relationships. Hierarchies are all around us—think of an organization chart where employees report to managers, who report to their managers, and so on. A self join allows you to represent these types of relationships within a table. For example, if an `employees` table has a column for `manager_id` (which references `employee_id`), a self join can show the reporting structure:

sql

Copy

```
SELECT e.employee_name, m.employee_name AS manager_name
```

43. `FROM employees e`
44. `LEFT JOIN employees m ON e.manager_id = m.employee_id;`
45.

This simple self join query shows each employee and their manager, which is essential when dealing with hierarchical data in one table.

46. **Indexing for join performance** is like tuning your car engine for better speed. Without proper indexing, MySQL will end up doing full table scans, which is about as efficient as trying to find your car keys in a junk drawer. When joining tables, ensure that the columns used in your join conditions are indexed. For example, if you're joining the `employees` table on `employee_id`, make sure `employee_id` is indexed in both tables. Proper indexing reduces the work MySQL has to do and speeds up the join process, making your queries run smoother and faster.

47. **Using UNION with joins** can be useful when combining results from multiple queries. Sometimes, you may want to run two queries that return similar data from different sources and combine them into one result set. A `UNION` can help you do this seamlessly. For instance:

sql

Copy

```
SELECT order_id, product_name FROM orders
```

48. `UNION`
49. `SELECT return_id, product_name FROM returns;`
50.

The `UNION` combines the results of both queries, while eliminating duplicates. This is like having two playlists for different moods, but combining them into one ultimate playlist.

51. **Handling NULL values in joins** requires a careful touch. When you join tables, you'll often encounter `NULL` values, especially when using `LEFT JOIN`. A `NULL` in the result means that no matching data was found in the right table. Handling this correctly can improve the quality of your results. For example:
sql
Copy

```
SELECT customer_name, order_id
```

52. `FROM customers c`
53. `LEFT JOIN orders o ON c.customer_id = o.customer_id`
54. `WHERE o.order_id IS NULL;`
55.

This query returns customers who have not placed any orders—ensuring that you don't just "assume" data exists but actually handle the absence of data gracefully.

56. **Dealing with complex relationships** is like solving a Rubik's cube. If you have many-to-many relationships, you'll need to model them with a **junction table**. A junction table stores the relationships between two other tables. For example, if you're dealing with students and courses, you might create a junction table like `student_courses` to track which students are enrolled in which courses. Then, you can perform multiple joins to get the full picture:
sql
Copy

```
SELECT s.student_name, c.course_name
```

57. FROM students s
58. JOIN student_courses sc ON s.student_id = sc.student_id
59. JOIN courses c ON sc.course_id = c.course_id;
60.

This solution allows you to properly model and retrieve data from complex many-to-many relationships.

61. **Best practices for complex joins** are essential to avoid slow queries and inefficient data retrieval. The first step is to minimize the number of rows involved in the join by filtering data early with a `WHERE` clause. The second step is to use indexing effectively, particularly on columns used in join conditions. Third, always limit the number of columns retrieved to what is necessary for your result. The more efficient your joins, the faster your queries will run. Lastly, be sure to keep your join conditions simple and logical. Like a good recipe, simplicity often leads to the best results.

62. **The LIMIT clause** can be your best friend when you need to restrict the number of rows returned. After executing a complex join, if you're just testing or only need a small subset of data, use `LIMIT` to avoid overwhelming your system with unnecessary data. For example:
sql
Copy

SELECT customer_name, order_id

63. FROM orders
64. LIMIT 10;
65.

This ensures that you're only working with the most relevant data, and it prevents the query from running too long.

66. **Avoiding unnecessary joins** can save your queries from spiraling into chaos. Each time you add a table to a join, you're asking MySQL to work harder. Before performing joins, ask yourself whether the data is truly necessary. If a table is irrelevant or provides redundant information, there's no need to include it. Reducing unnecessary joins simplifies your queries and makes your database more efficient.

67. **Joins with conditions and subqueries** can enhance the logic of your query, but they also come with performance costs. Subqueries in the `WHERE` clause, for example, can force MySQL to run the subquery multiple times. Instead of using subqueries, consider rewriting your query to use joins. This is a classic case of "less is more," where fewer, well-chosen joins often outperform complex subqueries.

68. **Transactions and joins** go hand in hand when performing multi-step data modifications. If you're joining data and making updates, it's important to wrap those queries in a transaction to ensure data consistency. For example, if you're transferring funds between two accounts, joining customer data and updating account balances, you want all operations to succeed or fail together. Using `START TRANSACTION` and `COMMIT` ensures that your operations are atomic and consistent.

69. **Optimizing large join queries** can be a challenge, but by splitting the queries into smaller, more manageable parts, you can improve performance. If you need to work with large datasets, consider breaking the query into temporary steps or using temporary tables to hold intermediate results. This approach keeps MySQL from trying to process everything in one go, which can slow things down significantly.

70. **Humor in SQL**: Finally, a little humor can go a long way when dealing with complex queries. Sometimes, the best way to troubleshoot a slow query is to ask yourself, "Do I really need this join, or am I just trying to impress my boss with how complicated this looks?" After all, good SQL queries are like good jokes—they should be simple, clean, and easy to follow.

71. **Conclusion**: Advanced joins and data relationships allow you to extract valuable insights from complex data, but they require practice and finesse. By understanding when and how to use self joins, multiple joins, composite joins, and subqueries, you can master even the most intricate data relationships. Armed with the knowledge of best practices, you'll optimize your queries to be both efficient and effective. Keep practicing, keep experimenting, and may your joins always be fast and your database always responsive!

Chapter 18: Views in MySQL: Simplifying Complex Queries

1. Let's talk about **views** in MySQL—a magical tool that can transform the most convoluted SQL queries into something sleek and easy to manage. Think of a view as a **virtual table** —it doesn't store data physically, but it gives you the ability to access complex queries as though they were a regular table. You could say a view is like a shortcut to your favorite coffee shop, allowing you to skip the long lines and get your favorite drink without all the hassle. For example, if you need to repeatedly join several tables, a view can save you from writing the same intricate `JOIN` statements over and over again. Creating views is like hiring an assistant who does all the heavy lifting while you sit back and relax. By the end of this chapter, you'll understand how views can clean up your queries, make your life easier, and let you focus on the fun stuff.

2. At its core, a **view** is a **stored query**. Unlike a table, which holds physical data, a view holds the SQL query itself. When you query a view, MySQL runs the query it's stored with and returns the results. It's like having a fancy, reusable recipe that you can call upon anytime without having to remember the ingredients and steps. To create a view, use the `CREATE VIEW` statement. For example, let's say we want to create a view that shows customer order details:
   `sql`

Copy

```
CREATE VIEW customer_order_details AS
```

3. `SELECT c.customer_id, c.customer_name, o.order_id, o.order_date`
4. `FROM customers c`
5. `JOIN orders o ON c.customer_id = o.customer_id;`
6.

Now, instead of writing this join every time, you can simply query the view like a table:
`sql`
Copy

```
SELECT * FROM customer_order_details;
```

7.

8. **Views are excellent for encapsulating complex queries**. If you have a query that involves multiple joins, unions, or subqueries, putting it into a view can simplify your life. It's like outsourcing the hard part of the work to someone else. For example, if you're dealing with a complicated query that involves multiple tables—such as `orders`, `customers`, `products`, and `employees`—creating a view makes the query simpler, and your code becomes more readable. The view hides the complexity, so all you have to do is refer to the view as if it were a regular table. Your co-workers will marvel at your newfound simplicity, and your future self will thank you.
9. One of the biggest advantages of using views is **reusability**. Let's face it: we all get tired of repeating ourselves. Instead of writing out the same SQL code in multiple places, you can define a view once and reuse it anywhere in your queries. It's like telling your database, "Hey, I wrote this awesome query already—don't make me write it again." This can be a huge time-saver, particularly in large projects or applications where you have complex reporting or data manipulation that requires the same base query. You're basically setting up a shortcut to access commonly used query results. Just make sure to give your view a **meaningful name**—it's hard to remember what `view1` does, but `customer_order_summary` is a little more self-explanatory.
10. **Views help with maintaining consistency**. When you have complex logic embedded directly in your queries, it can be easy for things to get out of sync. If you ever need to make a change—like modifying a calculation or updating a join—you only need to do it

in one place: the view definition. This ensures that the change propagates across all queries using that view. It's like making a change to a master recipe instead of modifying every individual dish. Instead of hunting down each query that uses that complex logic, you just update the view once. That's a win for consistency and sanity. The alternative is making 100 small, repetitive changes—sounds fun, right?

11. While views can make your queries easier to manage, there's one **catch** you need to be aware of: **performance**. Because views are essentially stored queries, they don't store data themselves. Every time you query a view, MySQL has to execute the underlying query and return the result. So, if the view is based on complex joins or aggregations, the performance can be a little sluggish, especially when working with large datasets. To avoid unnecessary performance hits, use views for queries that aren't performance-critical or for smaller, more straightforward queries. Views are like that friendly coworker who helps out—but if you keep asking them for coffee runs, they might get a little slow. Use views wisely!

12. **Updatable views** are another consideration. Not all views are updatable, meaning you can't just insert, update, or delete data in a view as if it were a regular table. To make a view updatable, you have to follow some restrictions. The underlying query must be simple (no joins, subqueries, or aggregation), and the columns involved should correspond directly to columns in the base tables. For example, you could create a view based on a single table and update that view:

    sql
    Copy

```
CREATE VIEW customer_names AS
```

13. `SELECT customer_id, customer_name FROM customers;`
14.

Now, you can update `customer_names`, and the changes will be reflected in the base table `customers`. But if you have a view involving complex joins or calculations, updating it directly is a no-go. You'll need to modify the underlying tables directly. It's like trying to make a change to a masterwork of art—you can't just slap a coat of paint on it and expect the same effect.

15. **Materialized views**—though not natively supported in MySQL—are like the secret sauce of optimizing query performance when working with large datasets. A materialized view stores the results of a query physically, just like a regular table. This means that when you query the materialized view, you're not executing the query again. You're simply reading from a precomputed table. The downside, of course, is that it requires manual updates to refresh the data in the materialized view. But if you're dealing with slow queries, a materialized view can save you a ton of time. Just don't go overboard with them, as they consume storage and need to be updated periodically.

16. If you find yourself needing to create multiple views to handle different segments of your data, be cautious about **view nesting**. Nesting views inside other views is like nesting Russian dolls—what starts simple can quickly get complex. While it's tempting to create a whole series of interconnected views, each level adds more processing time. The more layers you add, the slower the execution might become. It's easy to get carried away and think, "The more views, the better!" but sometimes you just need to simplify. MySQL's view system can handle some complexity, but don't ask it to do all the heavy lifting for you. Think of it as layering ingredients in a cake: keep it simple, and everything will turn out better.

17. **Using views for security** is another great application. You can restrict access to sensitive data by providing users with a view that only exposes the necessary columns. Let's say you have a `users` table with sensitive information like social security numbers. Instead of giving direct access to the full table, you can create a view that only shows the non-sensitive data, such as `user_id`, `first_name`, and `email`. This limits access to sensitive data, allowing you to enforce **data privacy** while still providing useful information to the user. It's like having a bouncer at the door—he lets people in, but only if they're here for the right reasons.

18. The process of **updating a view** is simple, but there's one crucial thing you need to know: any change to the view's definition requires you to **drop and recreate** it. Unlike regular tables, views aren't automatically updated with structural changes to the underlying data. For instance, if you add a new column to a table that the view relies on, you'll need to update the view to include that column. Think of it like updating your résumé—if your job description changes, you have to rewrite the whole thing. Fortunately, this process is simple, and once the view is recreated, your queries will reflect the new structure.

19. **Best practices** for using views include keeping them simple, using meaningful names, and avoiding overly complex queries. Remember, a view is meant to simplify your SQL—not complicate it further. If your view's SQL is too complex, it's doing more harm than good. Keep views for common tasks, like aggregating data or filtering out unnecessary columns, but leave the heavy-lifting queries for the raw tables. Don't use views as a crutch for sloppy query writing. Just because it's stored doesn't mean it's efficient.

20. Another great use case for views is **reporting**. Let's say you need to generate a weekly sales report that aggregates orders, customers, and products. You could write this complex query every time you need the report, or you could simply create a view that stores the query. This way, every time you need the report, you just query the view, and voila! Reports, served on demand. It's like having your favorite coffee ready every morning—no need to brew it yourself. With views, you get efficiency and a consistent result without the hassle.

Refreshing views is an important consideration, especially if the underlying data changes frequently. Since views don't store data themselves, you need to make sure the data they show is up-to-date. While MySQL doesn't support automatic refreshing of views, you can implement a manual refresh strategy by updating the view periodically or using scheduled events to update the data if necessary. Think of it like periodically cleaning the windows so you can see clearly—views won't refresh themselves unless you tell them to. In some cases, it might be more efficient to drop and recreate the view at scheduled intervals. If your underlying data is dynamic, though, you might want to reevaluate whether a view is the best approach, as you might end up querying data that isn't timely enough. To avoid this, look into using **materialized views** (though not directly supported in MySQL) or external caching mechanisms for frequent, heavy queries.

Performance considerations: Views might be convenient, but they can sometimes slow things down if you're not careful. If your view contains a complex query, each time you access the view, MySQL has to run that query again. If the query is very large, it can have a significant performance hit, especially with joins or aggregations. It's like using a shortcut to the grocery store that's lined with obstacles—you think it'll be faster, but it's actually a maze. Keep your views as simple as possible and avoid nesting views too deeply. The deeper the nesting, the more work MySQL has to do, like peeling layers off an onion. When optimizing views, remember: less is more. Complex views might be tempting, but they often cost you in performance.

View dependencies can sometimes be a little confusing. When you create a view that depends on other views or tables, you need to be mindful of how changes to those underlying structures might affect the view. If you drop or alter a base table that the view depends on, MySQL will throw an error when you try to query the view. This is like trying to watch a movie that's no longer available on streaming services—things just don't work as expected. Always keep an eye on view dependencies when modifying your database schema. If you decide to change the columns of a table or delete a column that a view relies on, be sure to update the view accordingly. Be aware of the chain reactions that might happen, and document those dependencies to avoid any surprises when schema changes occur.

As with anything in MySQL, there are **trade-offs** to using views. They're not always the best solution, and like every tool in your SQL toolbox, they should be used wisely. If your query is too complex or performance is critical, you might want to avoid views in favor of a more straightforward approach. Views should simplify your life, not add complexity. Know when to use them, and when to leave them in the toolbox. Think of views as your trusty Swiss Army knife: incredibly handy, but not meant to replace every tool in your collection. Use them for **repetitive** queries, **complex aggregations**, or situations where **security** is a concern, but don't use them when you can achieve the same result more efficiently with direct queries or temporary tables.

Debugging views can sometimes feel like trying to find a needle in a haystack. When something goes wrong with your view, the first thing you should check is whether the underlying query is valid. Is the query returning the expected results when executed by itself? If the underlying query works, but the view still doesn't, look for issues such as incorrect data types, missing columns, or complex joins causing trouble. Sometimes, you'll need to break down the query into smaller pieces and run them separately to pinpoint the problem. Debugging views can feel like an endless scavenger hunt, but at least with views, you're searching in a controlled environment. Always check your `EXPLAIN` output for insights on how MySQL is executing the query behind the view—if the query is slow, the problem might not be the view itself, but how MySQL is processing it.

Avoiding unnecessary joins in views is crucial. Views are fantastic for simplifying complex queries, but sometimes developers get a bit too carried away with joining multiple tables when it's not necessary. Imagine a recipe with 10 ingredients—delicious, sure, but a little over-the-top. Adding unnecessary joins to your views can introduce **complexity** without benefiting the final result. Keep it lean. Only include the tables and columns that are truly needed for the view's purpose. The less overhead, the faster your queries will run. Keep your view "recipe" simple—focus on what you need, and leave out the fluff.

Views and security go hand-in-hand. One of the best ways to protect sensitive data in MySQL is to use views to expose only the necessary columns. This is particularly useful when dealing with **personal** or **financial** information. By creating a view that excludes sensitive data, you can control what your users have access to without giving them full access to the underlying tables. For example, you could hide social security numbers, credit card details, or even employee salaries by using views to expose only the less-sensitive columns. It's like having a high-tech security gate around your database, only letting the right people see the right things. Use this technique to implement **role-based access control** and ensure your database complies with privacy regulations such as GDPR or HIPAA. If only the non-sensitive columns are exposed through the view, users won't even know what they're missing!

Combining views with stored procedures creates an incredibly powerful combination. Imagine building a house—you've got the views (the blueprints) and the stored procedures (the contractors making things happen). Views simplify complex data structures, while stored procedures let you encapsulate business logic, making your queries even more streamlined. Instead of combining all your logic into one giant query, break it down into manageable pieces: the view handles the data retrieval, and the stored procedure handles the business logic. This combination allows for reusable, modular code that can be updated more easily. The result? A more maintainable, flexible database system that can adapt to your needs as they change.

Complexity vs. simplicity: One of the most important things to keep in mind when working with views is the balance between complexity and simplicity. It's tempting to make a view that combines all sorts of complex logic, aggregations, and joins into one "catch-all" solution. But what happens when you need to troubleshoot? Now you have to dive into that complicated query again, and things get murky. Instead, try to create smaller, more focused views that each handle a specific task or data transformation. Think of them as building blocks. Simple views are easy to manage, debug, and reuse. When things get too complicated, you risk getting lost in the weeds—and believe me, no one wants that.

Limitations of views: While views are powerful, they do have limitations that you should be aware of. For example, not all views are **updatable**—meaning you can't perform `INSERT`, `UPDATE`, or `DELETE` operations on them unless the underlying query is simple and meets certain criteria. Views also can't take parameters, so if you need dynamic filtering, you might need to wrap a `SELECT` statement around the view or use a more flexible approach, like temporary tables. Furthermore, if your view depends on several large tables with complex joins, it might slow down your queries. It's like that time you tried to load 50 tabs in your browser—things slow down quickly when there's too much going on.

Best practices for views include keeping them simple, naming them clearly, and **documenting** their purpose. A well-named view is like a well-organized bookshelf—everything is easy to find, and you know exactly what each item is for. Avoid ambiguous names like `view1` or `tempview2`. Instead, give each view a descriptive name that reflects what data it encapsulates. For example, `monthly_sales_report` or `customer_order_summary` is much more intuitive than something generic. This not only helps with collaboration but also ensures that others can understand and reuse your views easily. Documentation is also important—explain the purpose of each view, any filters applied, and what users can expect from the results.

Conclusion: Views are one of the most powerful tools in your MySQL toolbox. They simplify complex queries, improve data consistency, and allow for easier security management. By using views to abstract away the complexity of your data, you can create reusable, clean queries that are easier to manage. However, as with all tools, it's important to use views wisely. Keep them simple, avoid unnecessary joins, and be mindful of performance. If you use views the right way, they will save you time, reduce complexity, and make your database work for you—just like a personal assistant who never takes a coffee break. So go ahead—simplify your queries, keep your database clean, and never look back!

Chapter 19: Triggers and Stored Procedures in MySQL

1. In this chapter, we're diving into the fascinating world of **triggers** and **stored procedures** in MySQL—two of the most powerful tools in your SQL arsenal. These features allow you to automate actions and encapsulate business logic directly within the database. Imagine not having to write the same logic over and over again in your application code—sounds like a dream, right? Well, triggers and stored procedures make that dream a reality. While they're both crucial for optimizing your database operations, they serve different purposes and can often complement each other beautifully. Think of triggers as your database's automatic response system, while stored procedures are the workhorses that can execute complex tasks on demand. Both will save you time and effort—like a good coffee machine, they just work better the more you know how to use them.

2. **What is a trigger?** A **trigger** is like a ninja that quietly works in the background, performing actions automatically when certain events occur in your database. It's a way to make MySQL respond to specific changes to your tables—whether it's an insert, update, or delete operation. For example, you might want to log every time a user updates their profile or automatically update the stock count after an order is placed. Instead of writing application code to track these changes, a trigger can take care of it for you. Triggers are fired automatically in response to events, so you don't have to worry about manually executing them. It's like setting your alarm to wake you up without ever having to hit snooze—reliable and hassle-free. Here's how you'd create a simple `AFTER INSERT` trigger:

   sql

Copy

```
CREATE TRIGGER log_insert
```

3. `AFTER INSERT ON orders`
4. `FOR EACH ROW`
5. `INSERT INTO order_logs (order_id, action) VALUES (NEW.order_id, 'Inserted');`
6.

7. **The three types of triggers** you'll encounter in MySQL are **BEFORE**, **AFTER**, and **INSTEAD OF** triggers. Each of these types defines when the trigger should be executed in relation to the operation (insert, update, delete). A **BEFORE** trigger runs before the operation is performed, allowing you to modify the data before it gets inserted or updated. An **AFTER** trigger runs after the operation has been completed, making it great for logging or taking further actions based on the results. The **INSTEAD OF** trigger is a bit of a rare bird—it replaces the action entirely, such as when you want to do something completely different instead of performing the insert, update, or delete. It's like telling your database, "I've got a better idea—let's do this instead!" When using triggers, make sure to understand the timing of each, so they don't clash or interfere with each other like a rock band tuning their instruments at the same time.

8. **Trigger syntax** is simple, but don't let that fool you—it's powerful! When creating a trigger, you'll need to specify the event that should fire the trigger (insert, update, or delete), the table the trigger should be applied to, and the action you want to take. MySQL also allows you to define **OLD** and **NEW** references, which represent the data before and after an update. For example, if you have a trigger that fires after an update, you can use `NEW` to refer to the new values being updated and `OLD` to refer to the old values. It's like being able to take a snapshot of data before and after a change, so you can make decisions based on the context of the operation. Here's a simple example:
   sql
   Copy

```
CREATE TRIGGER before_update_employee
```

9. `BEFORE UPDATE ON employees`
10. `FOR EACH ROW`
11. `BEGIN`
12. `  IF OLD.salary <> NEW.salary THEN`

13. INSERT INTO salary_changes (employee_id, old_salary, new_salary)
14. VALUES (OLD.employee_id, OLD.salary, NEW.salary);
15. END IF;
16. END;
17.

This trigger logs any salary changes before they're committed to the database. It's efficient, like a "before and after" shot in a fitness program, tracking progress at each step.

18. **Stored procedures**, on the other hand, are more like the *swiss army knife* of MySQL. They are precompiled blocks of code stored in the database, allowing you to execute complex logic without needing to repeatedly write it out in your queries. If you need to perform multiple SQL queries with certain business logic, a stored procedure is the way to go. They help keep your application code clean and reusable, just like how you wouldn't write out the same instructions for making spaghetti every time—you'd just have a standard recipe to refer to. The syntax for creating a stored procedure is:

sql

Copy

```
DELIMITER $$
```

19. CREATE PROCEDURE GetCustomerOrders(IN customer_id INT)
20. BEGIN
21. SELECT order_id, order_date FROM orders WHERE customer_id = customer_id;
22. END $$
23. DELIMITER ;
24.

This stored procedure takes a `customer_id` as an input and returns a list of their orders. You can call it like this:

sql

Copy

```
CALL GetCustomerOrders(101);
```

25.

Stored procedures let you bundle all the SQL logic into one neat package. It's like using a robot to make your coffee—push a button, and it does all the work.

26. **Stored procedures can also accept parameters**, making them more flexible than a pre-packaged query. You can define input parameters (for data you provide when calling the procedure) and output parameters (for data that comes back from the procedure). This allows you to create dynamic, reusable code. It's like giving your database a shopping list and asking it to return the items you requested—no need to type out each item individually. Here's an example of a procedure that accepts both an input and an output parameter:

sql

Copy

```
DELIMITER $$
```

27. `CREATE PROCEDURE GetEmployeeInfo(IN emp_id INT, OUT emp_name VARCHAR(100))`
28. `BEGIN`
29. `  SELECT name INTO emp_name FROM employees WHERE employee_id = emp_id;`
30. `END $$`
31. `DELIMITER ;`
32.

This procedure accepts an employee ID and returns the employee's name as an output parameter. When you call the procedure, you can use the output:

sql

Copy

```
CALL GetEmployeeInfo(1001, @emp_name);
```

33. `SELECT @emp_name;`
34.

35. **Triggers vs. stored procedures**—what's the difference, and when should you use which? It's like deciding whether to use a hammer or a screwdriver—both tools are useful, but for different jobs. Triggers are best for **automating actions** in response to events like data changes (inserts, updates, or deletes). They are reactive, automatically executing based on specific actions that occur in the database. Stored procedures, on the other hand, are like your personal *command center* for running **complex operations** on demand. If

you need to perform a sequence of actions or queries that might not be tied to a specific event, stored procedures are your best friend. Think of triggers as the automated background worker, and stored procedures as the decision-making CEO calling the shots when needed.

36. **The power of triggers** really shines when you need to maintain **data integrity**. For example, imagine you have a `stock` table and an `orders` table, and you want to ensure that the stock quantity is always updated whenever a new order is placed. Instead of manually updating stock levels in your application code, you can use a trigger to do this automatically every time a new order is inserted. It's like setting up a smart thermostat that adjusts the temperature automatically—no need to check it yourself.
    Here's an example of how you could do this with a `BEFORE INSERT` trigger:
    sql
    Copy

    ```
    CREATE TRIGGER update_stock
    ```

37. `BEFORE INSERT ON orders`
38. `FOR EACH ROW`
39. `BEGIN`
40. `  UPDATE stock`
41. `  SET quantity = quantity - NEW.quantity`
42. `  WHERE product_id = NEW.product_id;`
43. `END;`
44.

    Now, whenever a new order is placed, the stock quantity will update automatically. It's efficient and keeps things running smoothly behind the scenes.
45. **Stored procedures in action** can do far more than just retrieve data—they can execute multiple queries and even handle **business logic**. Suppose you want to perform a multi-step operation, like deducting money from one account, adding it to another, and logging the transaction. Instead of writing the same code in your application over and over, encapsulate it in a stored procedure:
    sql
    Copy

    ```
    DELIMITER $$
    ```

46. `CREATE PROCEDURE TransferFunds(IN from_account INT, IN to_account INT, IN amount DECIMAL)`

47. BEGIN
48. UPDATE accounts SET balance = balance - amount WHERE account_id = from_account;
49. UPDATE accounts SET balance = balance + amount WHERE account_id = to_account;
50. INSERT INTO transactions (from_account, to_account, amount) VALUES (from_account, to_account, amount);
51. END $$
52. DELIMITER ;
53.

Now you just call `TransferFunds` whenever you need to transfer money. It's like a money-transfer robot that never gets tired or forgets to log the transaction.

54. **Triggers and stored procedures are great for automating repetitive tasks**, but don't go overboard. Too many triggers can slow down your database, especially if you have a lot of insertions or updates happening frequently. It's like asking your robot to do too many chores at once—you might get the results, but it will take longer. Likewise, storing too much logic in stored procedures can make them hard to debug and maintain. Use triggers when you need things to happen automatically in response to database events, but keep stored procedures for more complex, multi-step operations. Balancing the two is like being a great chef—knowing when to let the sous-chef handle the prep work, and when you need to step in to create the final dish.

55. **Debugging triggers and stored procedures** can be a little tricky because you can't just run them directly like a regular query. When things go wrong, MySQL doesn't give you the same error messages you might expect with standard SQL queries. For stored procedures, you can use **CALL** to test them and check for any errors:

sql
Copy
```
CALL TransferFunds(101, 102, 50.00);
```
For triggers, debugging can be more challenging because they're fired automatically based on events. One strategy is to log the actions inside the trigger by inserting data into a log table. For example, you can create a log table to track trigger actions:

sql
Copy
```
CREATE TABLE trigger_log (
  log_id INT AUTO_INCREMENT PRIMARY KEY,
  action_time DATETIME DEFAULT CURRENT_TIMESTAMP,
  action_description VARCHAR(255)
);
```

12. **Transaction control with stored procedures** is essential when you're working with operations that need to be atomic. Imagine you're transferring funds between accounts—if something goes wrong halfway, you don't want money to disappear into the void. A stored procedure can handle this by using **transactions** to ensure that either all steps are completed successfully or none at all. Here's an example:

sql
Copy
```
DELIMITER $$
CREATE PROCEDURE TransferFundsAtomic(IN from_account INT,
IN to_account INT, IN amount DECIMAL)
BEGIN
  START TRANSACTION;
  UPDATE accounts SET balance = balance - amount WHERE
account_id = from_account;
  UPDATE accounts SET balance = balance + amount WHERE
account_id = to_account;
  COMMIT;
END $$
DELIMITER ;
```

The `START TRANSACTION` and `COMMIT` statements ensure that the whole operation is treated as one atomic unit. If something goes wrong, you can use `ROLLBACK` to undo the changes.

13. **Nested stored procedures** are a fun concept that allows you to call one stored procedure from within another. It's like having one task delegate a subtask to another task. For example, imagine you have a stored procedure to process customer orders, but it calls another stored procedure to handle inventory updates. This makes your code modular and reusable. Here's an example:

sql
Copy
```
CREATE PROCEDURE ProcessOrder(IN order_id INT)
BEGIN
  CALL UpdateInventory(order_id);
  CALL GenerateInvoice(order_id);
END;
```

You can call `ProcessOrder` to execute both `UpdateInventory` and `GenerateInvoice`. It's like outsourcing small, related tasks to specialists, keeping everything tidy and efficient.

14. **Error handling in stored procedures** is essential for ensuring that your database operations run smoothly. In MySQL, you can use **`DECLARE CONTINUE HANDLER`**

to handle errors gracefully. Instead of letting the procedure fail unexpectedly, you can set up custom error handling to manage the situation. Here's an example:

sql

Copy

```
DELIMITER $$
CREATE PROCEDURE TransferFundsWithErrorHandling(IN
from_account INT, IN to_account INT, IN amount DECIMAL)
BEGIN
  DECLARE EXIT HANDLER FOR SQLEXCEPTION
  BEGIN
    ROLLBACK;
    SELECT 'An error occurred during the transaction.';
  END;
  START TRANSACTION;
  UPDATE accounts SET balance = balance - amount WHERE
account_id = from_account;
  UPDATE accounts SET balance = balance + amount WHERE
account_id = to_account;
  COMMIT;
END $$
DELIMITER ;
```

This procedure will rollback the transaction if there's an error and display a custom error message. Think of it as putting a seatbelt on your stored procedures to ensure they don't crash in case of unexpected bumps.

15. **Triggers and performance** go hand-in-hand, but they need to be handled carefully. Triggers can slow down data modifications, especially if they contain complex logic or if they fire frequently. Be cautious of writing triggers that perform heavy operations, like large `INSERT` or `UPDATE` queries, since these will be executed every time the triggering event happens. It's like having a traffic jam every time you want to go out—eventually, it's going to cause delays. Optimize your triggers by keeping them lightweight and efficient.

16. **Transaction control in triggers** is a powerful feature. You can use **BEGIN, COMMIT, and ROLLBACK** within triggers to control transactions. However, this feature is available only in **AFTER triggers**, as BEFORE triggers run before the transaction is committed and are not transaction-controlled. If you need to ensure that changes across multiple tables happen together, using **transaction control within triggers** can help maintain consistency, but be mindful of performance.

17. **Scheduling stored procedures** in MySQL can be done using **events**, which allow you to run a stored procedure at specific intervals. Events are like your personal scheduler,

running procedures at times you define. For example, you might want to update inventory levels at midnight, or generate a report every Sunday:

sql
Copy
```
CREATE EVENT update_inventory_event
ON SCHEDULE EVERY 1 DAY
DO
  CALL UpdateInventory();
```
Events are great for automating periodic tasks and ensuring that important procedures are executed without any manual intervention.

18. **Testing triggers and stored procedures** thoroughly is crucial for ensuring they work as expected. The key to avoiding disasters is to test your triggers in a **development environment** first. Make sure they handle edge cases, such as null values or invalid data, before deploying them to production. Similarly, stored procedures should be tested with a variety of inputs to ensure they behave correctly. Testing is like rehearsing a play—you want everything to go smoothly on opening night.

19. **Best practices for triggers** include keeping them simple, focusing on one task, and ensuring they don't interfere with other processes. Triggers are not a place to put complicated business logic or long-running queries. If you find yourself writing a trigger that's doing too much, it's a good idea to break the task into smaller pieces. Triggers should be there to automate specific actions that need to happen in the background without bogging down the database.

20. **Best practices for stored procedures** include keeping them modular, easy to maintain, and well-documented. As your database grows, so does the potential for complexity. When writing stored procedures, avoid embedding excessive logic within them. Instead, focus on creating procedures that are concise and focused on performing specific tasks. This makes it easier to troubleshoot and update them down the road. Documentation is key—if someone else (or your future self) needs to modify the procedure later, clear comments explaining the purpose and function of each part will save time and frustration. Think of stored procedures as your personal manual—write it clearly, so others don't get lost trying to figure out what you did!

21. **Error handling in triggers** is often overlooked, but it's essential for ensuring that your data remains consistent. If a trigger encounters an error, the operation that fired it will continue as if nothing happened. This can cause unexpected issues, especially when performing actions that require strict data integrity. You can use the **`SIGNAL`** statement to raise an error within a trigger, which can help catch issues before they propagate. For instance, if you're trying to update a `stock` table and there's not enough inventory, you could raise an error:

sql
Copy

```
CREATE TRIGGER check_inventory
BEFORE UPDATE ON orders
FOR EACH ROW
BEGIN
  IF NEW.quantity > (SELECT stock_quantity FROM inventory
WHERE product_id = NEW.product_id) THEN
    SIGNAL SQLSTATE '45000' SET MESSAGE_TEXT = 'Not enough
stock available';
  END IF;
END;
```

This trigger will prevent the update and raise an error if there's insufficient stock, keeping your data integrity intact. Error handling in triggers might not be glamorous, but it's like putting a seatbelt on your database—it keeps things safe.

22. **Managing complex business logic with triggers** can sometimes be a tricky dance. While triggers are perfect for automating simple actions, like logging changes or updating stock levels, they become cumbersome when used for complex business logic. Triggers can start to interact unpredictably with one another if multiple triggers modify the same data, especially when they fire on the same event. This is where you need to keep a close eye on **order of execution**. If one trigger modifies data that another trigger depends on, things can quickly spiral out of control. In such cases, it might be better to use a **stored procedure** to handle the business logic, as stored procedures give you more control over the flow of operations. Think of it like coordinating a dance performance—every dancer needs to know when to enter and exit the stage to avoid stepping on each other's toes.

23. **Triggers and stored procedures** both work well in tandem. When you use triggers and stored procedures together, you can automate workflows that span multiple operations while maintaining a high level of control over how and when things happen. For example, a trigger can automatically insert a record into a log table every time an order is placed, while a stored procedure handles the actual business logic of processing that order. By combining the automation of triggers with the flexibility of stored procedures, you can create a well-oiled, automated data workflow that makes your database work smarter, not harder. It's like building a team of workers, each with a specific task, all contributing to the overall success of the operation.

24. **Security considerations for triggers and stored procedures** are important. Since both triggers and stored procedures run with the privileges of the user who created them, you need to ensure that the privileges are granted appropriately. You don't want a trigger to accidentally modify data it shouldn't, or a stored procedure to be executed by someone who doesn't have the right access. To mitigate these risks, be sure to **restrict access** to the creation and execution of stored procedures and triggers. Use **role-based access control** to grant permissions only to trusted users who need to interact with these objects. Think of this like locking up a safe—only let the right people have the keys.

25. **Conclusion**: Triggers and stored procedures are indispensable tools in MySQL that can significantly simplify complex tasks, improve performance, and enhance security. Triggers allow you to automate operations in response to specific database events, while stored procedures let you encapsulate logic and execute it on demand. By using these features wisely, you can reduce redundancy, enforce business rules, and keep your database running smoothly. Just remember that while triggers and stored procedures are powerful, they also come with their own challenges, especially when it comes to debugging and performance. Keep them clean, modular, and efficient, and they'll make your database work harder for you. With triggers handling the automatic background tasks and stored procedures handling the complex logic, you'll have a database that's as efficient and well-organized as a finely tuned orchestra.

Chapter 20: Backing Up and Restoring MySQL Databases

1. In the world of databases, **backups** are like insurance policies. You hope you'll never need to use them, but when disaster strikes, you'll be glad you have one. Whether you're dealing with a hardware failure, human error, or just an unfortunate series of events involving a coffee spill and a server restart, **backing up your MySQL databases** is an essential part of database administration. In this chapter, we'll cover the ins and outs of backing up and restoring MySQL databases, because without solid backup practices, your data could be one server crash away from oblivion. Think of your backup strategy as the "save game" function in a video game—only instead of losing a few hours of progress, you might lose everything. So, let's get prepared and set up a backup system that'll save you from the database equivalent of hitting the "I lost everything" button.

2. **Why back up your database?** The answer is simple: **data loss is a nightmare**. Whether it's a sudden server crash, a corrupted table, or a mistakenly executed `DROP DATABASE`, once your data is gone, it's gone. You can't simply "Ctrl+Z" your way out of it, no matter how much you wish you could. It's like forgetting to save your work and losing all your edits—except in the case of MySQL, it's more like losing the whole project. **Regular backups** provide a safety net, ensuring you can restore your data to a previous state in the event of an emergency. If you've ever faced data loss without a backup, you know the feeling of horror that comes with realizing your data is irretrievably gone. Backups are your lifeline, your parachute in case the unthinkable happens.

3. **Types of backups**: When it comes to MySQL, you've got a few different backup options, and the right choice depends on your specific needs. **Logical backups** are typically done using `mysqldump`—a tool that extracts your database into a plain-text SQL file. This file contains all the SQL statements necessary to recreate your database, including table structures, data, and indexes. It's like making a photocopy of your entire database, and it's great for small to medium-sized databases. On the flip side, **physical backups** involve copying the actual database files (e.g., `.ibd`, `.frm`, and `.myd` files), which is a bit more efficient for large databases, as it doesn't require dumping the data into SQL format. Physical backups are faster, but they tend to be a little less flexible, especially

when it comes to restoring individual tables. It’s like choosing between a detailed photocopy and a quick snapshot—you can decide based on how much detail you need.

4. **Using `mysqldump` for logical backups**: The most common method for backing up a MySQL database is using the `mysqldump` utility. This tool creates a text file containing all the SQL commands needed to recreate the database, including its structure and data. It’s a handy tool, like a Swiss Army knife for backup and restore operations. Here's a simple command to back up a database:
   bash
   Copy

```
mysqldump -u root -p database_name > backup.sql
```

5. This command backs up `database_name` and stores it as `backup.sql`. It’s a one-liner that does the trick—no complicated setup or configuration needed. However, if you’re backing up a database with a lot of data, the file can grow large, and it might take a while to process. But fear not! You can also compress the output to save space:
   bash
   Copy

```
mysqldump -u root -p database_name | gzip >
backup.sql.gz
```

6. This will create a compressed backup file that’s smaller and easier to store.
7. **Backing up multiple databases**: If you need to back up more than one database, `mysqldump` has you covered. You can specify multiple database names in one command to back them all up at once:
   bash
   Copy

```
mysqldump -u root -p --databases db1 db2 db3 >
backup_multiple.sql
```

8.

The `--databases` flag tells `mysqldump` to back up all the specified databases. This is like having one backup tool that gathers all your precious data in one neat package. However, keep in mind that this approach creates a single backup file for all your databases, so if you need to restore one specific database later, you'll need to extract it from the backup file.

9. **Backing up the entire MySQL server**: In certain situations, you might want to back up **all the databases** on your server. This is where the `--all-databases` flag comes in handy. If you're about to upgrade MySQL or perform maintenance on the server, it's wise to back up the entire database server:

bash

Copy

```
mysqldump -u root -p --all-databases >
all_databases_backup.sql
```

10.

This will back up every database on the MySQL server, including system databases like `information_schema`, `performance_schema`, and `mysql`. While this is convenient, be cautious about restoring all databases at once, as some system databases might not need to be restored if you're just restoring user data.

11. **Scheduling regular backups**: One of the most critical steps in **backup strategy** is ensuring that you back up your database regularly. After all, backing up once every six months won't do much if your database is updated daily. To automate this process, you can schedule regular backups using cron jobs on Linux or Task Scheduler on Windows. Here's an example of a cron job to back up your database every night at midnight:

bash

Copy

```
0 0 * * * mysqldump -u root -pYourPassword
database_name > /path/to/backup/backup_$(date +\%F).sql
```

12.

This cron job runs the backup at midnight and saves it with the current date in the filename (`backup_YYYY-MM-DD.sql`). Setting up automated backups ensures you don't have to remember to do it manually, and it also reduces the chances of forgetting or being lazy. It's like setting a reminder to brush your teeth—you'll do it automatically, and your database will stay healthy.

13. **Using binary logs for point-in-time recovery**: While `mysqldump` backups are great for full backups, they don't allow you to restore to a specific point in time. If you need to restore your database to an exact moment (like five minutes before a disaster struck), binary logs are your friend. Binary logs record all changes to your database, including inserts, updates, and deletes. To use binary logs, you need to enable them in your MySQL configuration file (`my.cnf` or `my.ini`):
    ini
    Copy

    ```
    [mysqld]
    ```

14. `log-bin = /var/log/mysql/mysql-bin.log`
15.

    After enabling binary logs, you can use them to **replay** database changes up to a specific point in time, helping you recover data without restoring the entire backup. It's like having a time machine for your database, allowing you to reverse or fast-forward to a point when everything was working fine.

16. **Physical backups with `xtrabackup`**: If you're working with a **large database**, logical backups might not be fast enough or efficient. This is where **physical backups** come into play, and the tool you want to use is **Percona XtraBackup**. XtraBackup is a hot backup utility, meaning it can back up your database while it's still running, without locking the tables. It's like sneaking into the kitchen and stealing cookies without anyone noticing. To use XtraBackup, you simply install the tool and run:
    bash
    Copy

    ```
    xtrabackup --backup --target-dir=/path/to/backup
    ```

17.

    This creates a backup of your database files without interrupting database operations. It's fast and efficient—perfect for handling larger datasets.

18. **Restoring from `mysqldump` backups** is a breeze. Once you've created a backup using `mysqldump`, restoring it is as simple as running the SQL commands from the backup file. Use the `mysql` command to load the data back into MySQL:

bash
Copy

```
mysql -u root -p database_name < backup.sql
```

19.

This command will recreate the entire database, including its structure and data. It's like pressing "undo" in your favorite text editor, but with the entire database. Just make sure the target database already exists, or create it with:

sql
Copy

```
CREATE DATABASE database_name;
```

20.

21. **Restoring from binary logs** allows you to perform **point-in-time recovery**. After restoring from a backup, you can apply changes from the binary logs to bring the database back to its exact state at a specific time. You'll first need to restore the full backup and then apply the binary logs to replay the changes:

bash
Copy

```
mysqlbinlog /var/log/mysql/mysql-bin.000001 | mysql -u
root -p
```

22.

This will replay all the changes in the binary log, allowing you to roll your database forward to the point in time you need. It's a bit like restoring a save file, then using the history to rewind or fast-forward to the moment everything went wrong (or right).

23. **Restoring physical backups** with `xtrabackup` is also pretty straightforward. XtraBackup provides a script to prepare the backup before restoring it. After running the backup, you need to prepare the backup data (this ensures the transaction logs are applied correctly), then restore it to the MySQL data directory:

bash

Copy

```
xtrabackup --prepare --target-dir=/path/to/backup
```

24. `cp -R /path/to/backup/* /var/lib/mysql/`
25.

Once copied, restart MySQL, and the backup will be fully restored. Just like a well-prepared meal, the process is efficient and smooth, ensuring your database is served hot and ready to go.

26. **Restoring a single table** is often overlooked but necessary in some cases. If you don't need to restore the entire database, and only need to recover one table, you can extract that table from your `mysqldump` backup and restore it separately. It's a bit like rescuing a single sock from the laundry pile—no need to rewash the entire load. To restore a specific table, extract it from the full backup:
bash
Copy

```
sed -n '/^CREATE TABLE `table_name`/,/UNLOCK TABLES/p'
backup.sql > table_backup.sql
```

27. `mysql -u root -p database_name < table_backup.sql`
28.

29. **Backup verification** is essential to ensure that your backups are **restorable** when you need them. Backing up your database is only half the battle; you also need to regularly verify that your backups are actually usable. Performing a test restore on a separate system or environment can help catch any potential issues early. It's like checking the parachute before you jump—you want to be sure it works. Ideally, you should do this periodically, even if everything seems fine, to ensure the integrity of your backups.

30. **Cloud backups** are a convenient solution for ensuring your data is safe off-site. Many MySQL users opt to back up their databases to cloud services like **Amazon S3**, **Google Cloud Storage**, or **Azure Blob Storage**. Using cloud storage for backups provides an extra layer of protection, ensuring your data is safe even if your physical servers are compromised. To automate cloud backups, you can integrate `mysqldump` with cloud upload tools like AWS CLI:
bash
Copy

```
mysqldump -u root -p database_name | gzip | aws s3 cp -
s3://your-bucket-name/backup.sql.gz
```

31.

Cloud backups are secure, scalable, and accessible from anywhere—just don't forget the password to your cloud storage!

32. **Backup strategies** should include not only full backups but also **incremental backups**. Full backups capture everything, but they can take up a lot of storage space. Incremental backups only capture changes since the last backup, making them more efficient and quicker to execute. By combining full and incremental backups, you create a balanced strategy that ensures quick recovery while minimizing storage usage. It's like having a full-sized spare tire but keeping a compact one for emergencies.

33. **Backup retention** is an often overlooked aspect of managing backups. Having too many backups lying around is like hoarding old gadgets that you'll never use. You don't want to store endless versions of backups, consuming valuable disk space. Establish a **retention policy** that dictates how long backups are kept and when they should be deleted. For example, you might keep full backups for a week and incremental backups for a month, automatically cleaning up older backups to free up space.

34. **Automated monitoring of backups** is another critical step. It's easy to forget to check if your backups are actually running, especially if you've scheduled them to run automatically. Set up email notifications or monitoring tools to alert you if a backup fails, so you can take action quickly. Think of it as the backup's personal assistant—making sure everything runs smoothly without you having to constantly check up on it.

35. **Backup encryption** is essential if you're dealing with sensitive data. You don't want your backups floating around in the cloud or on a physical drive without encryption, especially if you're working with personally identifiable information (PII), financial data, or other confidential content. Use tools like **GPG** or MySQL's built-in encryption options to encrypt your backups before storing them. It's like locking your valuables in a safe—adding an extra layer of protection, just in case.

36. **Backup strategies for high-availability systems** like **replication** and **clustering** require a bit more thought. If you're running a MySQL **replication setup** or a **Galera Cluster**, your backup strategy needs to take into account the distributed nature of your data. You can still use `mysqldump` or `xtrabackup`, but be mindful of the fact that your data is being replicated across multiple nodes. Ensure that you back up all nodes to avoid inconsistencies, and consider using **Galera's integrated backup tools** for more advanced setups.

37. **Disaster recovery planning** should be a key part of your backup strategy. The point of backing up your data is not just to have a copy, but to have a plan for how to restore it when things go wrong. Document your restoration process step by step, so that when disaster strikes, you're not fumbling around in the dark. A disaster recovery plan is like having an emergency evacuation route—when the alarms go off, you know exactly where to go.

38. **Backup monitoring dashboards** can be helpful for large environments. Tools like **Percona Monitoring and Management (PMM)** or **Zabbix** can help you visualize the health of your backups, alert you to failures, and track the status of your backup jobs. Think of these tools as your backup's fitness tracker—ensuring everything is running at peak performance.

39. **Testing backups** periodically ensures that you're not living in an illusion of safety. You can't just back up and forget about it; you need to periodically test your ability to restore from backups. You don't want to find out after a disaster that your backup is corrupted or incomplete. Schedule regular test restores in a development or staging environment to confirm that your backups are functional and your recovery process is smooth.

40. **Backup documentation** might seem like overkill, but it's a lifesaver when you're under pressure. Keeping detailed documentation of your backup procedures and configurations is essential. If something goes wrong, you won't have time to remember all the steps. With clear documentation, you can restore a backup quickly, confidently, and without unnecessary stress. It's like having a user manual for your car's engine—when things break, you'll know exactly where to look.

41. **Conclusion**: Backing up and restoring MySQL databases isn't the most glamorous part of database administration, but it's one of the most important. A well-thought-out backup strategy protects your data from unforeseen disasters and ensures that you can restore your database quickly and efficiently when needed. Whether you're using `mysqldump` for logical backups or `xtrabackup` for physical backups, always remember to schedule regular backups, encrypt sensitive data, and test your recovery process. Like a good insurance policy, a reliable backup strategy gives you peace of mind and protects you from the worst-case scenarios. Just like the saying goes, "Better safe than sorry"—especially when it comes to your precious data!

Chapter 21: MySQL Security Best Practices

1. Welcome to the world of **MySQL security**, where the phrase "better safe than sorry" is not just advice—it's a lifestyle. In this chapter, we'll dive into the **best practices** for securing your MySQL database, ensuring that your data is protected from unauthorized access, malicious actors, and even accidental deletions. If you've ever spent a sleepless night wondering whether your database is as secure as it should be, you're not alone. But fear not! We're here to walk you through practical, actionable steps to keep your data safe and sound, like a fortress of code. The goal isn't just to secure your database but to make sure you're also equipped to handle any security challenges that may arise. Think of this

chapter as your ultimate guide to putting up the best locks, fences, and firewalls to guard your data—without turning into a paranoid database administrator who checks the locks every five minutes.

2. **The first rule of MySQL security is: never use the default password**. MySQL comes with default root user access during installation, and while it might be convenient to get started, this is like leaving the keys to your house in the mailbox with a "help yourself" sign. Changing the default password should be the very first step you take after installing MySQL. A strong password is crucial—make sure it's long, contains a mix of letters, numbers, and special characters, and doesn't resemble anything remotely related to your cat's name or your birthday. For example, `root12345` isn't a great choice, but `9!Xe@2dbPm!z`—now that's a password to write home about. Also, consider using a password manager to keep track of these beastly passwords. After all, if your database security was a locked door, the last thing you want is to hand out the spare key.

3. **Limit access to the MySQL server**. MySQL allows you to configure which hosts can connect to the server, and it's crucial to restrict access only to those that need it. By default, MySQL listens on all interfaces, which means any device with network access can try to connect (unless you've set firewalls). It's like leaving your garage door wide open to the street—anyone passing by could pop in and take a look around. You can limit which IP addresses are allowed to connect to the MySQL server by configuring the `bind-address` directive in your `my.cnf` file. This tells MySQL to only accept connections from specific hosts, reducing the surface area for potential attacks. A firewall is another important layer, preventing unauthorized access by blocking unwanted connections before they even reach MySQL.

4. **Use least privilege access** when setting up users and granting permissions. Just as you wouldn't give a stranger your house keys without a background check, don't give database users more permissions than they need. The principle of **least privilege** means only granting the minimum required access for users to perform their tasks. Create users with only the privileges they need, such as `SELECT` for read-only users, or `INSERT` for users who need to add records, and nothing more. You can always grant additional privileges later if necessary, but this is much safer than starting with an overly permissive user. For example, creating a user who can `SELECT` from a table without the ability to `UPDATE` or `DELETE` can prevent some serious mistakes.

5. **Avoid using the root user for everyday tasks**. The `root` user in MySQL is the database equivalent of an all-powerful admin, but that doesn't mean you should use it to check your email or write blog posts. It's a best practice to create specific users with restricted privileges for everyday tasks. If you're working on a web app that only needs to read from a database, don't give it `root` access—create a user that only has `SELECT` privileges. It's like giving your web app a driver's license that only allows it to drive in the slow lane. If you're concerned about losing the root password, store it securely (and not in plaintext on the server).

6. **Enable SSL encryption** to protect data during transmission. It's important to ensure that any data exchanged between the MySQL server and clients is secure, especially when dealing with sensitive information. By using **SSL/TLS encryption**, you can prevent data from being intercepted by hackers during transmission, a technique known as **Man-in-the-Middle (MitM) attacks**. Enable SSL encryption in your MySQL configuration to ensure that all communication is encrypted and cannot be easily eavesdropped on. To implement SSL, you'll need to create certificates, configure MySQL to use them, and then require clients to connect using SSL. It's like putting your database conversations in a secure, soundproof box to keep unwanted ears from listening in.

7. **Secure MySQL with firewalls**. A **firewall** acts as a barrier between your MySQL server and the outside world, controlling who can and cannot access your database. You can configure a firewall to only allow specific IP addresses or subnets to connect to your MySQL server, blocking unwanted traffic before it even has a chance to enter. This is especially important if your MySQL server is exposed to the internet. Think of a firewall as a **bouncer**—it checks IDs at the door and only lets in the folks who belong there. Firewalls such as **iptables** or **UFW** (Uncomplicated Firewall) are great for limiting access, and they work well in combination with restricting `bind-address` in MySQL.

8. **Regularly update MySQL**. One of the simplest yet most effective ways to keep your database secure is to stay on top of updates and patches. MySQL releases security updates to address vulnerabilities and bugs, and running an outdated version of MySQL is like using outdated antivirus software—it's just asking for trouble. Set up automatic updates or establish a regular schedule for checking and applying updates to ensure that your server is always running the latest, most secure version of MySQL. It's like regularly servicing your car to make sure it doesn't break down in the middle of nowhere.

9. **Audit your database activity** using the MySQL Enterprise Audit plugin or other logging mechanisms. **Auditing** allows you to keep track of who's doing what on your MySQL server. Did a user execute a `DROP TABLE` command? Was someone sneaking around with `UPDATE` commands? Audit logs record all these actions, so you can spot any suspicious behavior. This is like having a security camera in your database's "room" that keeps track of every movement. Setting up regular audits is an essential part of ensuring that only authorized users are making changes to your database.

10. **Use secure backups**. You wouldn't want to store your backup copies in an unsecured, easily accessible location, so why would you do the same with your database backups? Ensure your backups are stored in a secure location, whether that's an encrypted cloud storage service or a secure local server. You can also use **backup encryption** to make sure that even if someone gets access to the backup files, they can't easily read the data. It's like locking your backup data in a safe deposit box, ensuring that it's protected even if your primary database is compromised. To add another layer of security, limit access to the backup files to only trusted administrators.

11. **Disable symbolic-links**. MySQL allows you to use symbolic links (symlinks) to point to files in other directories. While this can be convenient for certain configurations, it can also be a security risk, especially when the `symlink` feature is enabled by default. Attackers can exploit this feature to gain access to unauthorized files on your server, so it's a good idea to **disable symbolic-links** in your MySQL configuration file (`my.cnf`) by setting:

```
ini
Copy
symbolic-links=0
```

This simple configuration change can prevent malicious users from taking advantage of symlinks to access sensitive files outside of MySQL's designated directories.

12. **Log file security** is just as important as securing the data itself. MySQL logs can contain a wealth of sensitive information, from query details to login attempts. It's essential to ensure that the MySQL log files are **readable only by trusted administrators** and that the log files are stored in a secure location. You can also configure **log rotation** to prevent log files from growing too large and consuming disk space. It's like hiding the journal of your actions in a locked drawer so that only authorized individuals can access it. Don't let your logs become the open book for hackers.

13. **Secure MySQL configuration** by tweaking some important security settings in your `my.cnf` file. First, ensure that **`skip-networking`** is enabled, so MySQL doesn't listen for remote connections unless explicitly required. By default, MySQL listens on all network interfaces, which can expose your database to potential attacks. Also, avoid using the default `localhost` user and instead, create specific users for local and remote access. Additionally, make sure you limit `root` access to local connections only, so no one can remotely access the root account over the network.

14. **Use role-based access control** (RBAC) to further enhance security. MySQL 8.0 introduced **roles** as a way to simplify the management of user privileges. With RBAC, you can create predefined roles like `DBA`, `Developer`, or `Analyst` and assign users to these roles, rather than granting individual privileges. This makes it easier to enforce security policies and ensures that users only have access to what they need. Think of it like assigning job titles with specific access rights instead of giving everyone a "superpower" when they don't need it.

15. **Avoid default configurations** that may leave your MySQL server exposed. When you install MySQL, the default settings might not be the most secure, especially for production environments. The **default user accounts**, especially the `root` account, often have excessive privileges, and **default configurations** might leave certain features open to attacks. Always review and customize the MySQL configuration files after installation to harden your MySQL server. It's like unpacking a new appliance and reading the instruction manual—make sure it's set up the right way before you start using it.

16. **Monitor MySQL processes** for suspicious activity. Just as you monitor your house with security cameras, you should also monitor MySQL's processes to ensure that nothing suspicious is happening. MySQL provides a number of tools to help you track and monitor database activity, including the **`SHOW PROCESSLIST`** command, which lists all active queries and connections. Keep an eye on long-running queries, unknown users, or other anomalies that might indicate a security issue. It's like having a watchful eye on your database—preventing intruders from slipping through unnoticed.

17. **Prevent SQL injection attacks** by using parameterized queries. SQL injection is one of the oldest tricks in the hacker's book, and it's still incredibly effective if you're not careful. By using **prepared statements** and **parameterized queries**, you can ensure that user input is treated as data, not executable code. This is like asking a security guard to search every bag before entry, ensuring no dangerous items sneak through the door. Many MySQL libraries, including those for PHP, Python, and Java, support parameterized queries, so there's no excuse for leaving your database open to this attack.

18. **Monitor user access** carefully. Regularly review the **permissions** granted to MySQL users to make sure that no one has more access than they need. Over time, users may change roles, departments, or projects, and their access should be adjusted accordingly. Don't leave old permissions lying around like abandoned vehicles. Periodically audit and **revoke unnecessary privileges**—it's like cleaning out the attic and getting rid of things you don't need anymore. Over-privileged users are like open windows in your database's security—someone could crawl through and cause trouble if you're not paying attention.

19. **Enforce password complexity** to ensure that user credentials are strong and difficult to crack. MySQL allows you to configure password policies to enforce rules like minimum length, complexity, and expiration. A weak password policy is like leaving the door wide open for attackers to stroll right in. You can configure password policies using the **`validate_password`** plugin, which requires users to set strong passwords. This plugin checks passwords against specific criteria, ensuring that they're tough to guess. If you want to ensure your MySQL server isn't an easy target, start by demanding stronger passwords.

20. **Disabling symbolic-links** can prevent attackers from exploiting symbolic link features to gain access to unauthorized files on your server. In addition to the obvious security benefits, disabling symbolic-links can help ensure that MySQL doesn't accidentally cross boundaries and access files that should remain off-limits. By setting the following option in your MySQL configuration file, you're essentially telling MySQL, "Don't even think about using symlinks":

```
ini
Copy
symbolic-links=0
```

21. **Regularly back up your database**—but we can't emphasize this enough. Security breaches aren't the only way to lose data; hardware failures and human errors happen too. A solid backup strategy ensures that if disaster strikes, you can restore your database to a

safe state. Combine **logical and physical backups** to cover all your bases and make sure your backups are stored securely—preferably off-site or in the cloud. No one likes to think about data loss, but a regular, tested backup schedule is like a spare tire—you hope you never need it, but you'll be glad you have it when the time comes.

22. **Use external security tools** to enhance MySQL security. While MySQL provides some built-in security features, don't rely on them as your only line of defense. Tools like **Fail2ban**, which helps block malicious IPs after a certain number of failed login attempts, and **intrusion detection systems (IDS)**, can add an extra layer of protection. It's like having a backup security team that watches your database 24/7, ensuring no one is trying to sneak in through the back door.

23. **Encrypt your backups**. If you store backups on physical devices or in the cloud, make sure those backups are **encrypted**. Encryption ensures that even if an attacker gains access to your backup files, they won't be able to make sense of the data. This step is especially important for **sensitive data** like personally identifiable information (PII) or financial records. Use tools like **GPG** or MySQL's built-in encryption functions to protect your backup files, so they're safe from prying eyes.

24. **Apply patches** regularly to your operating system and MySQL installation. Database security doesn't end with MySQL itself—ensure that your operating system and other software components are up to date with the latest security patches. Vulnerabilities in the OS can expose your database to attack, so a comprehensive security approach means applying patches to **everything** in your stack. Think of your database server like a house—patching holes in the roof and walls ensures you don't get unexpected visitors.

25. **Conclusion**: Securing MySQL is not a one-time task—it's an ongoing process. By following the best practices we've outlined, such as limiting user access, enabling SSL encryption, backing up your data, and keeping your software up-to-date, you'll be well on your way to ensuring that your database is both secure and efficient. Remember, database security is all about reducing the risk and making it as hard as possible for attackers to gain unauthorized access. And with these tips in hand, your MySQL server will be ready to withstand anything thrown its way—because, just like a ninja, it's better to be prepared and stealthy than to be caught off guard!

Chapter 22: Advanced MySQL Functions and Features

1. Welcome to the realm of **advanced MySQL functions and features**, where the magic happens and your queries evolve from basic SELECTs into powerful, optimized, and specialized database operations. This chapter is for those of you who have mastered the basics and are eager to take your MySQL skills to the next level. We're diving into the deep end, exploring advanced functions, powerful features, and creative ways to manipulate and extract data that will make your queries faster, cleaner, and more efficient. By the end of this chapter, you'll have a toolbox full of powerful techniques that will elevate your SQL game—think of it like going from a bicycle to a sports car in the world of databases. We'll cover everything from window functions to full-text search, stored procedures to advanced joins—so buckle up, it's going to be an exciting ride.

2. **Window Functions** are one of the most exciting additions to MySQL in recent years, and they've really revolutionized the way we perform analytics. Unlike traditional aggregate functions, which collapse the result set to a single value, window functions allow you to compute over a set of rows while retaining the individual rows in the result. It's like taking a snapshot of the entire dataset but giving each row the ability to see the bigger picture. For example, if you want to calculate a running total or rank rows in a dataset, window functions are your best friend. Here's a simple example using the `ROW_NUMBER()` function:

sql

Copy

SELECT customer_id, order_id, amount,

3. ROW_NUMBER() OVER (PARTITION BY customer_id ORDER BY order_date) AS row_num

4. FROM orders;

5.

This assigns a row number to each order for each customer, allowing you to rank their purchases. It's like giving each order a ranking badge without collapsing the table.

6. **Rank and dense_rank** are two of the most common window functions used to assign ranks to rows based on certain criteria. `RANK()` gives ranks to rows with the same value, but it leaves gaps in the ranking, while `DENSE_RANK()` gives consecutive ranks without gaps. This distinction can be important when you need to assign ranks based on performance, like in a competition leaderboard. For example:

sql

Copy

SELECT student_id, score,

7. RANK() OVER (ORDER BY score DESC) AS rank,

8. DENSE_RANK() OVER (ORDER BY score DESC) AS dense_rank

9. FROM students;

10.

This will give you both ranking systems, showing how students perform relative to one another. `RANK()` might leave gaps if multiple students have the same score, while

`DENSE_RANK()` ensures that no rank is skipped. It's like being given a choice between two ways to rank your friends based on how much pizza they ate—both are valid, but one might have fewer gaps.

11. **Full-text search** in MySQL is another fantastic feature for working with text data. If you need to search through large volumes of text and return results based on relevance, full-text search is your best option. By creating a full-text index on columns containing text, you can use MySQL's `MATCH()` and `AGAINST()` functions to search for keywords and rank results by relevance. It's like being able to search for keywords in a giant book and having MySQL tell you exactly where the good stuff is. For example:
    sql
    Copy

    ```
    SELECT article_id, title
    ```

12. `FROM articles`
13. `WHERE MATCH(title, content) AGAINST ('+database +performance' IN BOOLEAN MODE);`
14.

    This will return articles that mention both "database" and "performance," with more relevant results appearing first. Full-text search is great for websites, blogs, or any application that needs to find specific terms in large bodies of text quickly.

15. **Stored Procedures** are one of the most powerful features in MySQL, allowing you to encapsulate complex business logic and execute it on demand. Stored procedures help keep your SQL code clean, reusable, and centralized, so you don't have to rewrite the same queries over and over again. When you need to perform multiple steps that involve querying and manipulating data, a stored procedure is the way to go. For example, you might want to perform a set of updates on a user's profile and order history in one go:
    sql
    Copy

    ```
    DELIMITER $$
    ```

16. `CREATE PROCEDURE UpdateUserProfile(IN user_id INT, IN new_email VARCHAR(100))`
17. `BEGIN`
18. `  UPDATE users SET email = new_email WHERE id = user_id;`
19. `  UPDATE orders SET email = new_email WHERE user_id = user_id;`

20. END $$
21. DELIMITER ;
22.

This stored procedure lets you update the user's email and all related orders with a single call. Stored procedures give you a cleaner way to encapsulate logic that's used in multiple places, ensuring consistency and reusability.

23. **Triggers** in MySQL are like your database's watchdog, constantly observing and reacting to changes in the data. Triggers can be set to automatically execute when certain events occur, such as an insert, update, or delete operation. For example, if you want to automatically update a last-modified timestamp every time a record is updated, a trigger can handle it:

    sql
    Copy

    CREATE TRIGGER update_last_modified

24. BEFORE UPDATE ON users
25. FOR EACH ROW
26. SET NEW.last_modified = NOW();
27.

This trigger ensures that every time a user record is updated, the `last_modified` column is automatically set to the current timestamp. It's like setting an alarm to go off every time something important happens—so you don't have to worry about it.

28. **Views** are another great MySQL feature that allows you to simplify complex queries by encapsulating them into a virtual table. A view is a stored query that can be treated like a regular table in your queries. They're great for simplifying repetitive queries or hiding the complexity of joins. For example, if you frequently need to access customer orders with some basic aggregation, you can create a view to handle that:

    sql
    Copy

    CREATE VIEW customer_order_summary AS

29. SELECT customer_id, COUNT(order_id) AS total_orders, SUM(amount) AS total_spent
30. FROM orders

31. GROUP BY customer_id;
32.

Now, you can simply query the `customer_order_summary` view instead of repeating the aggregation logic every time. It's like having a custom-built report that's always available at your fingertips.

33. **CROSS JOIN** is an often-overlooked but interesting join in MySQL. While `INNER JOIN` and `LEFT JOIN` are more commonly used, a **CROSS JOIN** produces the Cartesian product of two tables, meaning it combines each row from the first table with every row from the second table. This can be useful in certain scenarios, such as when generating all possible combinations of two sets of data. For example:

    sql
    Copy

    ```
    SELECT color, size
    ```

34. FROM colors
35. CROSS JOIN sizes;
36.

This query will return every combination of colors and sizes, so if you have three colors and four sizes, you'll get 12 rows. But beware—CROSS JOINs can lead to very large result sets if the tables involved have a lot of data. It's like trying to find every possible combination of ice cream toppings—delicious, but potentially overwhelming.

37. **The GROUP_CONCAT() function** is another powerful tool for aggregation in MySQL. While GROUP BY is great for summarizing data, sometimes you might want to combine multiple rows of data into a single value, like concatenating all the names of the people who attended an event. That's where GROUP_CONCAT() comes in:

    sql
    Copy

    ```
    SELECT event_id, GROUP_CONCAT(attendee_name ORDER BY
    attendee_name ASC) AS attendees
    ```

38. FROM event_attendees
39. GROUP BY event_id;
40.

This will give you a comma-separated list of attendee names for each event, which is handy when you want to present data in a more readable format. It's like having a party guest list that automatically organizes itself—no more manual counting!

41. **JSON support** in MySQL is a feature that makes working with JSON data a breeze. With MySQL 5.7 and later, MySQL supports **native JSON data types**, allowing you to store and manipulate JSON directly in the database. This is particularly useful for modern applications that deal with dynamic, schema-less data. For example, you can store a user's preferences as a JSON object:

sql

Copy

```
CREATE TABLE users (
42.   user_id INT PRIMARY KEY,
43.   preferences JSON
44. );
45.
```

You can then query and update the JSON data using built-in functions:

sql

Copy

```
SELECT user_id, JSON_EXTRACT(preferences, '$.theme') AS
theme
46. FROM users;
47.
```

JSON support makes MySQL a powerful tool for handling unstructured data, allowing you to store and retrieve JSON objects just like any other data type.

48. **MySQL Partitioning** is a technique that can be used to divide a large table into smaller, more manageable pieces, or partitions. This can improve performance by limiting the amount of data that needs to be scanned for queries that filter on the partition key. Partitioning is like breaking down a massive novel into smaller chapters, making it easier to read and navigate. MySQL supports several types of partitioning, including **range partitioning**, **list partitioning**, and **hash partitioning**:

sql

Copy

```
CREATE TABLE sales (
49.   sale_id INT,
50.   sale_date DATE,
51.   amount DECIMAL(10, 2)
52. )
53. PARTITION BY RANGE (YEAR(sale_date)) (
54.   PARTITION p2019 VALUES LESS THAN (2020),
55.   PARTITION p2020 VALUES LESS THAN (2021)
56. );
57.
```

This partitions the `sales` table by year, storing records from 2019 and 2020 in separate partitions, which can improve performance for queries filtering on `sale_date`.

58. **MySQL replication** allows you to create copies of your MySQL database across multiple servers, ensuring high availability and fault tolerance. Replication is useful when you want to distribute the load or create backups of your data in real-time. You can set up a **master-slave replication** where the master server handles all writes and the slave servers replicate the data for read operations:

ini

Copy

```
[mysqld]
59. server-id=1
60. log-bin=mysql-bin
61.
```

This makes MySQL an excellent choice for scaling applications, as read traffic can be distributed across multiple servers. It's like having a team of clones handling the workload—each one doing its part to keep things running smoothly.

62. **Foreign Keys** are one of the most useful tools for enforcing data integrity in MySQL. By using foreign keys, you ensure that relationships between tables are maintained and that data isn't accidentally corrupted. For example, if you have an `orders` table and a `customers` table, a foreign key ensures that every order is linked to an existing customer:

sql

Copy

```
CREATE TABLE orders (
63.   order_id INT PRIMARY KEY,
64.   customer_id INT,
65.   FOREIGN KEY (customer_id) REFERENCES
customers(customer_id)
66. );
67.
```

Foreign keys prevent you from adding data that doesn't make sense (like an order without a customer), ensuring that your database remains **consistent** and **reliable**.

68. **Auto-incrementing columns** are another helpful feature when you want MySQL to automatically generate unique IDs for new rows. This is useful for tables where each row needs a unique identifier, such as order IDs or user IDs. You simply define a column with the `AUTO_INCREMENT` attribute, and MySQL will take care of the rest:
sql
Copy

```
CREATE TABLE users (
69.   user_id INT AUTO_INCREMENT PRIMARY KEY,
70.   name VARCHAR(100)
71. );
72.
```

Now, every time you insert a new user, MySQL automatically generates a unique ID for them. It's like having a numbered ticket at a concert—no need to manually assign IDs!

73. **Advanced Joins** are another powerful feature that enables you to combine data from multiple tables. While you've probably used `INNER JOIN` and `LEFT JOIN`, MySQL also supports **RIGHT JOIN**, **OUTER JOIN**, and **SELF JOIN** for more complex data retrieval. These joins allow you to extract data from multiple related tables in a single query. For example:
sql
Copy

```
SELECT a.name, b.order_date
```

74. FROM customers a
75. LEFT JOIN orders b ON a.customer_id = b.customer_id;
76.

This LEFT JOIN returns all customers, even those who haven't placed an order, while matching order data when available. Joins are like the "glue" that holds your data together —without them, everything would fall apart.

77. **Transaction handling** in MySQL ensures that your database maintains consistency even in the event of a failure. A transaction allows you to group multiple SQL queries together and either commit them all at once or roll them back if something goes wrong. This is like making sure that your bank transaction is only processed if all steps are successful—if one step fails, the entire transaction is undone. To use transactions, simply wrap your queries in START TRANSACTION, COMMIT, and ROLLBACK:

sql

Copy

```
START TRANSACTION;
```

78. UPDATE account SET balance = balance - 100 WHERE account_id = 1;
79. UPDATE account SET balance = balance + 100 WHERE account_id = 2;
80. COMMIT;
81.

82. **MySQL Event Scheduler** allows you to schedule tasks to run at specific intervals, like cron jobs but within MySQL. Events are useful for tasks like periodic data cleanups, automatic backups, or running reports. To create an event, simply enable the event scheduler and define the task you want to run:

sql

Copy

```
CREATE EVENT clean_up_old_data
```

83. ON SCHEDULE EVERY 1 DAY

84. DO
85. DELETE FROM logs WHERE log_date < NOW() - INTERVAL 30 DAY;
86.

This event will automatically delete logs older than 30 days every day. It’s like setting a recurring appointment for MySQL to keep things tidy and organized.

87. **Temporary tables** are incredibly useful for breaking down complex queries. You can create a temporary table to store intermediate results, allowing you to simplify subsequent queries. The table only exists during the session, so once the session is over, it’s automatically deleted. It’s like having a clutter-free desk—use it while you need it, then clear it off when you're done:
sql
Copy

CREATE TEMPORARY TABLE temp_sales AS

88. SELECT product_id, SUM(amount) AS total_sales
89. FROM sales
90. GROUP BY product_id;
91.

92. **MySQL partitions** improve performance by breaking large tables into smaller, more manageable pieces. Partitioning is great for dealing with large datasets where you often filter based on specific column values. For example, if you have a sales table, you could partition it by year:
sql
Copy

CREATE TABLE sales (

93.   sale_id INT,
94.   sale_date DATE,
95.   amount DECIMAL(10, 2)
96.)
97. PARTITION BY RANGE (YEAR(sale_date)) (
98.   PARTITION p2020 VALUES LESS THAN (2021),
99.   PARTITION p2021 VALUES LESS THAN (2022)

100.);
101.

This will make queries that filter by year faster, as MySQL can access just the relevant partition.

102. **The `EXPLAIN` command** is a powerful tool for understanding how MySQL executes your queries. It shows you the execution plan, helping you identify slow queries and optimize them. By analyzing the output of `EXPLAIN`, you can see if MySQL is using the right indexes or performing unnecessary full table scans. This is like a diagnostic tool for your queries—giving you a peek under the hood:

sql
Copy

```
EXPLAIN SELECT * FROM orders WHERE customer_id = 100;
```

103.

104. **Using `IFNULL()` and `COALESCE()`** functions helps you handle `NULL` values in your queries. These functions are useful when you want to replace `NULL` with a default value, preventing unwanted gaps in your results. For example:

sql
Copy

```
SELECT product_id, IFNULL(discount, 0) AS discount FROM
products;
```

105.

This replaces any `NULL` discount values with 0, ensuring that you don't end up with incomplete or misleading data.

106. **Regular expressions** in MySQL allow you to search for complex patterns in your data. If you've ever needed to find a specific string within a column but didn't want to use basic `LIKE` patterns, `REGEXP` is your go-to function. For example, if you want to find all phone numbers in a specific format, use:

sql
Copy

```
SELECT phone_number

107.FROM contacts
108.WHERE phone_number REGEXP '^[0-9]{3}-[0-9]{3}-[0-9]
    {4}$';
109.
```

This will return only phone numbers in the format `123-456-7890`. It's like searching for a needle in a haystack, but with a finely-tuned magnet.

110. **The `UUID()` function** generates a universally unique identifier (UUID) that can be used to uniquely identify records across databases and systems. This is especially useful in distributed systems where you want to ensure that records have a globally unique identifier, even if they come from different servers. For example:
sql
Copy

```
INSERT INTO users (id, name) VALUES (UUID(), 'Alice');

111.
```

UUIDs are great for generating identifiers in systems that need to sync data across multiple locations.

112. **Data masking** in MySQL allows you to obfuscate sensitive data when displaying it. If you need to show part of the data but want to keep certain values hidden for privacy or security reasons, you can use functions like `CONCAT()` and `SUBSTRING()` to mask data. For example, to display the last four digits of a credit card number:
sql
Copy

```
SELECT CONCAT('XXXX-XXXX-XXXX-', SUBSTRING(card_number,
13, 4)) AS masked_card

113.FROM customers;
114.
```

115. **MySQL's SET operations** allow you to combine multiple result sets using operations like `UNION`, `INTERSECT`, and `EXCEPT`. These are useful for combining or comparing data from multiple queries. For example, `UNION` combines results from two queries into a single result set, removing duplicates:

sql

Copy

```
SELECT product_name FROM products
```

116. UNION
117. SELECT product_name FROM discontinued_products;
118.

This returns all product names, combining the data from two different sources. It's like creating a playlist by merging two sets of songs into one smooth mix.

Chapter 23: MySQL Replication: Scaling Your Database

1. Welcome to the world of **MySQL replication**, where scaling your database is as easy as making copies—only without the paper jams! If you've ever found your database becoming the bottleneck in your application, you're not alone. As your system grows, so does the load on your database server, and suddenly, what was once a well-oiled machine starts wheezing like an old bicycle with a flat tire. Replication is the solution—MySQL's built-in mechanism to copy data from one server (the **master**) to one or more servers (the **slaves**). It's like having a team of database clones working together to spread the load and make sure no single server is overburdened. In this chapter, we'll break down how replication works, why you need it, and how to set it up. Grab your helmet, because we're about to scale your database to the next level.

2. **What is MySQL replication?** Simply put, replication is the process of copying data from a master MySQL server to one or more slave servers. This means that every time a change is made on the master, those changes are automatically replicated to the slave servers. This allows you to offload read queries to the slaves, keeping the master server free for write operations. Think of it like having a lead singer (the master) and backup singers (the slaves)—the lead singer does the hard work of writing new songs (inserts, updates), while the backup singers help with the performance by handling all the singing (read queries). By distributing the load, replication helps prevent performance bottlenecks and ensures your application runs smoothly even as the traffic ramps up.

3. **Types of replication** in MySQL come with their own flavors, so it's important to know which type suits your needs. The most common type is **master-slave replication**, where one server acts as the master (handling writes) and the others act as slaves (handling reads). There's also **master-master replication**, where two servers act as both master and slave, replicating each other's data. This can be useful for load balancing, but it requires

careful management to prevent conflicts. Think of it like two chefs in the kitchen—each is cooking up a storm, but you need to make sure they don't start adding the wrong ingredients to each other's dishes. MySQL also supports **circular replication** and **group replication**, which are used in more advanced setups for high availability.

4. **Setting up master-slave replication** is not as complicated as it sounds, but it does require some attention to detail. First, you need to configure the master server to allow replication and enable binary logging. Binary logging records all changes to the database, allowing the slave servers to replay those changes. On the master server, you'll need to enable binary logs in the `my.cnf` file:
   ini
   Copy

   ```
   [mysqld]
   ```
5. `log-bin = mysql-bin`
6. `server-id = 1`
7.

   This sets up the master to record all changes in the binary log and gives the server a unique ID (required for replication). Once you've done that, you'll need to create a replication user with the necessary privileges:
   sql
   Copy

   ```
   CREATE USER 'replica_user'@'%' IDENTIFIED BY 'password';
   ```
8. `GRANT REPLICATION SLAVE ON *.* TO 'replica_user'@'%';`
9.

   This ensures that the slave servers can connect and replicate data from the master.
10. **Configuring the slave** is the next step. On the slave server, you'll need to configure it to connect to the master and start replicating data. You'll edit the `my.cnf` file on the slave server and set a unique `server-id` for the slave, like so:
    ini
    Copy

```
[mysqld]
```

11. `server-id = 2`

12.

Then, on the slave, you'll tell it which master to connect to and provide the replication credentials:

sql

Copy

```
CHANGE MASTER TO
```

13. `  MASTER_HOST = 'master_ip',`
14. `  MASTER_USER = 'replica_user',`
15. `  MASTER_PASSWORD = 'password',`
16. `  MASTER_LOG_FILE = 'mysql-bin.000001',`
17. `  MASTER_LOG_POS = 4;`
18.

This connects the slave to the master server and tells it where to start reading the binary log from. You can find the `MASTER_LOG_FILE` and `MASTER_LOG_POS` by checking the master's binary log file and position before starting the replication process.

19. **Starting replication** is as simple as running the following command on the slave server:

sql

Copy

```
START SLAVE;
```

20.

This command tells the slave to start pulling data from the master and applying the changes. Once replication is running, you can check the status with:

sql

Copy

```
SHOW SLAVE STATUS\G
```

21.

This will display the current replication status, including whether the slave is running smoothly or has encountered any issues. It's like checking the engine lights on your car—if everything's running fine, you're good to go.

22. **Monitoring replication** is critical to ensure that your slave servers are up-to-date and in sync with the master. The `SHOW SLAVE STATUS` command provides a wealth of information, including the `Seconds_Behind_Master` field, which tells you how far behind the slave is from the master. Ideally, you want this number to be as close to zero as possible. If the slave falls too far behind, it could indicate performance problems, network issues, or high latency. It's like having a backup performer who keeps missing their cues—time to tune things up and get them back on track!

23. **Replication lag** is an issue that can occur if the slave falls behind in applying changes from the master. This can happen if the slave server is overloaded with read queries or if the master is making too many changes too quickly. Replication lag can result in outdated data on the slave, causing inconsistencies between the master and slave databases. To minimize lag, make sure the slave servers are adequately sized to handle the read load and that they have sufficient resources, like CPU and memory. It's like trying to get a slow runner to keep up with a speeding train—you need to give them the right tools to stay in the race.

24. **Replication filters** can be used to control which databases or tables are replicated to the slave. If you only want to replicate a subset of the data, you can specify replication filters in the `my.cnf` file on the slave:

ini

Copy

```ini
replicate-do-db = my_database
```

25.

This ensures that only the specified database will be replicated to the slave. Replication filters allow you to fine-tune what data is replicated, reducing unnecessary data transfer and saving on resources. Think of it like only inviting your friends who like the same pizza toppings to your party—keeping things simple and efficient.

26. **Troubleshooting replication** can sometimes feel like solving a mystery. If replication is broken or lagging, you'll need to carefully investigate the `SHOW SLAVE STATUS` output for clues. Common issues include network failures, replication errors, and

permissions problems. If you see errors like `Last_SQL_Error` or `Slave_IO_Running: No`, it's time to roll up your sleeves and dig deeper. One common issue is encountering duplicate entries when data has been modified on both the master and slave—this is where conflict resolution techniques come into play. It's like tracking down a criminal—when you find the problem, it's time to bring the culprit to justice!

27. **Master-Master replication** involves two servers that replicate to each other, creating a bi-directional replication setup. This setup is great for high availability and load balancing, as both servers can handle both read and write operations. However, master-master replication requires careful attention to avoid **write conflicts**. If both masters are updating the same data, it can cause data inconsistencies. To avoid this, you can use **auto-increment offsets** to ensure each server generates different primary key values, thus preventing key collisions. It's like two chefs in a kitchen—if they each use different ingredients and tools, they won't step on each other's toes.

28. **GTID-based replication** (Global Transaction Identifiers) is an improvement over traditional replication, as it provides a more reliable and flexible way to track changes. With GTID replication, each transaction is assigned a unique identifier, making it easier to track and manage replication between master and slave. This can help you avoid problems like **replication position errors** and **slave lag**. GTID-based replication simplifies failover scenarios, as it ensures that each transaction is applied in the correct order across all servers. It's like giving each transaction a unique barcode, ensuring that it's tracked properly from start to finish.

29. **Replication and high availability** go hand in hand. MySQL replication can be used as part of a high-availability architecture, ensuring that if one server fails, another can take over without disrupting service. By using **MySQL Cluster** or combining replication with **ProxySQL** or **MHA (MySQL High Availability)**, you can automate failover and recovery processes. In the event of a failure, the system can automatically promote a slave to become the new master, keeping your application online with minimal downtime. It's like having a backup quarterback ready to step in whenever your starter gets injured.

30. **MySQL Replication and load balancing** are a natural fit. By offloading read operations to slave servers, you can reduce the load on your master and ensure that your application can handle high traffic volumes. Tools like **ProxySQL** or **HAProxy** can be used to intelligently route read queries to the slaves and write queries to the master. This helps distribute the load and improves overall performance, especially for read-heavy applications. It's like having a well-coordinated team of servers, each playing to their strengths.

31. **Semi-Synchronous replication** is a variation of MySQL replication that adds an extra layer of safety. With **synchronous replication**, the master waits for at least one slave to acknowledge the transaction before it commits. This ensures that the data is replicated immediately, reducing the risk of data loss in case the master fails. However, it can

introduce some performance overhead, as the master must wait for confirmation from the slave. It's like asking for a receipt every time you make a purchase—extra safe, but it might slow you down a bit.

32. **Replication filters** also come in handy when you need to selectively replicate certain databases or tables. For example, if you have a large database but only need to replicate a subset of data to the slaves, you can specify **replication filters** to limit what gets copied. You can also use **`replicate-ignore-db`** to exclude certain databases from being replicated, which can be useful if you're replicating large databases that don't need to be available on the slave. It's like sorting your laundry by color before washing it—keeping everything neat and organized.

33. **Replication and backups** are another critical part of your high-availability strategy. While replication can help reduce the load on your master server and provide redundancy, it's not a substitute for regular backups. Regular backups are still essential to protect your data against corruption or accidental deletion. Always back up both the master and slave servers regularly, and test your backup strategy to ensure that you can restore from it if needed. It's like having both a spare tire and a jack—both are essential in case of an emergency.

34. **Replication with failover** is a powerful way to ensure high availability in MySQL. Failover is the process of automatically switching to a backup server if the primary server fails. You can configure MySQL replication to automatically detect when the master goes down and promote a slave to become the new master. Tools like **MHA (MySQL High Availability)** and **Orchestrator** can help manage this process, making failover seamless and automatic. It's like having a backup driver ready to take over when the first driver gets stuck in traffic.

35. **Replication delay** is an issue that can arise when the slave falls behind the master, causing data to be out of sync. Replication delay can occur when the slave server is under heavy load, network latency is high, or the master is producing a large volume of changes. To minimize delay, ensure that your slave servers have sufficient resources and that your network connection is fast and stable. It's like trying to catch up with a friend who's already way ahead of you—sometimes you need to pick up the pace.

36. **Managing replication with MySQL Enterprise** provides additional tools for monitoring and optimizing replication. MySQL Enterprise offers features like **Replication Monitor** and **Performance Schema** to track replication status, latency, and performance issues. These tools help you keep an eye on the health of your replication setup, ensuring that everything is running smoothly and efficiently. It's like having a dashboard to monitor the health of your car—knowing exactly when to service it.

37. **GTID-based replication** also provides greater flexibility and reliability. GTID (Global Transaction Identifier) replication tracks transactions with unique IDs, ensuring that each transaction is applied in the correct order across all servers. This makes it easier to recover from failures and ensures consistency across your database servers. GTID is especially useful in scenarios where you need to perform **failover** or **recovery** in

complex replication setups. It's like having a GPS to navigate your way through a complex route—no more getting lost.

38. **Data consistency** in MySQL replication is crucial for maintaining a healthy database ecosystem. When using replication, it's important to monitor the health of the slaves to ensure they are in sync with the master. MySQL's **`SHOW SLAVE STATUS`** and **`SHOW MASTER STATUS`** commands are invaluable for tracking replication progress and spotting any discrepancies. It's like keeping a checklist of things to do—if anything is off, you can quickly address the issue before it becomes a problem.

39. **Write conflicts in replication** can arise in a master-master replication setup, where both masters handle write operations. If the same data is modified on both servers simultaneously, it can cause inconsistencies. To handle write conflicts, you can use conflict resolution strategies such as **auto-increment offsets**, where each master generates different values for auto-increment fields, preventing key collisions. It's like coordinating two people working on the same project—making sure they don't step on each other's toes.

40. **Monitoring replication** with tools like **ProxySQL**, **MHA**, or **Orchestrator** is crucial for ensuring that replication is running smoothly. These tools offer advanced features like automated failover, load balancing, and replication monitoring, helping you maintain a healthy MySQL environment. ProxySQL, for instance, can intelligently route read and write queries to the appropriate servers, optimizing performance and ensuring that replication is always up to date. It's like having a traffic cop directing traffic to the right lanes—ensuring everything runs efficiently.

41. **Conclusion**: MySQL replication is an essential tool for scaling your database and ensuring high availability. Whether you're using master-slave, master-master, or GTID-based replication, it's critical to configure, monitor, and maintain replication effectively to avoid performance bottlenecks and data inconsistencies. With the right tools and techniques, replication can help you distribute the load, optimize read performance, and provide backup in case of failure. So, go ahead—scale your database with confidence, and remember, when it comes to replication, more is often better, as long as you're managing it well.

Chapter 24: Managing Large Databases in MySQL

1. Welcome to the big leagues, where your MySQL database has grown beyond a handful of tables and a few thousand rows. As databases grow larger, they start behaving like a rock concert—more fans, more noise, and more chaos. Managing large databases is not for the faint of heart, but don't worry; with the right tools, strategies, and a little know-how, you'll have everything under control. This chapter is all about **managing large databases** in MySQL, ensuring that they perform well, are easy to maintain, and scale efficiently as your data needs increase. We'll cover everything from optimizing queries to partitioning tables, to making sure your database is resilient and can handle growth

without falling apart. So grab your coffee, tighten your shoes, and let's dive into the world of managing MySQL databases on a much larger scale.

2. **Optimizing queries** is one of the first places to start when dealing with a large database. Queries that run fine with a small dataset can become sluggish as the data grows. Indexing is your best friend here. An index allows MySQL to quickly locate and retrieve data without scanning the entire table, which is crucial when you have millions of rows. Think of it like a high-speed internet connection—without it, everything takes forever, but with it, you can access data in a snap. However, **indexing too much** is like buying a warehouse full of books and labeling every single page—unnecessary and inefficient. Carefully choose which columns need indexing, and make sure they're really beneficial for your most frequent queries. Use **EXPLAIN** to analyze your queries and determine if indexes are being used effectively.

3. **Partitioning** is another powerful tool for managing large tables in MySQL. Partitioning allows you to break large tables into smaller, more manageable pieces, called partitions. Each partition stores a subset of the table's data, making it faster to query and easier to manage. Imagine trying to find a single page in a book that's the size of a skyscraper—partitioning breaks that book into chapters, making it easier to find the page you need. MySQL supports several types of partitioning, including **range**, **list**, **hash**, and **key** partitioning. For example, if you have a sales table with millions of records, you can partition it by year, so queries filtering on `sale_date` can be much faster. Partitioning can greatly improve performance, but be mindful of its complexity and how it affects queries that need to span across partitions.

4. **Sharding** is another technique used to scale large databases, especially when partitioning alone isn't enough. Sharding involves splitting your database into smaller, independent databases, each storing part of the data. Unlike partitioning, where data is split across different physical segments of a single table, sharding splits the database across multiple servers, each with its own set of data. This allows you to distribute the load and handle more queries in parallel, which is like having multiple lanes on a highway instead of just one. For example, if you have a global user base, you might shard the user data by region, placing each region's data on a different server. While sharding can be incredibly powerful for horizontal scaling, it introduces complexity, especially when it comes to data consistency and maintaining relationships across shards. So, treat sharding like a rocket launch—exciting, but requiring careful planning.

5. **Query caching** is an often-overlooked feature in MySQL that can significantly improve performance, especially for read-heavy workloads. MySQL can cache the results of SELECT queries and reuse them when the same query is executed again, saving valuable processing time. This is particularly useful when your database handles repetitive queries —like generating reports or fetching frequently accessed data. It's like finding the perfect shortcut to your favorite website instead of typing the URL every time. However, caching isn't always the right solution for every query. If your data changes frequently, caching might end up serving outdated results. Use **query cache** carefully, and ensure that the cache is invalidated when data changes to avoid serving stale data to users.

6. **Handling large datasets** requires special attention to **transaction management**. With large databases, you're more likely to experience long-running transactions that lock up resources and slow down the system. Break large transactions into smaller chunks to reduce locking time and improve concurrency. This is like unloading a delivery truck full of boxes—you don't want to unload it all at once, but instead, unload a few boxes at a time so you don't block traffic. For example, if you're updating a million records, consider batching the updates into smaller transactions. This reduces the strain on your server and helps maintain performance across all operations.

7. **Backups and restore strategies** become critical when you're managing a large database. A single failure can lead to significant data loss, and restoring large databases can be a time-consuming and complex task. Use **incremental backups** in addition to full backups, which capture only the changes since the last backup. This will allow you to perform quicker backups and restores. For example, instead of backing up your entire database every night, take a full backup once a week and incremental backups every day. This strategy ensures you can restore the database to any point in time without the performance hit of backing up the entire dataset every night. It's like having a backup parachute for every backup you take—you'll always have a safe landing if something goes wrong.

8. **Monitoring and alerting** are crucial for identifying and resolving performance issues before they affect users. As your database grows, it becomes harder to keep an eye on every query and metric manually. That's where **monitoring tools** like **Percona Monitoring and Management (PMM)**, **MySQL Enterprise Monitor**, or **Prometheus** come in handy. These tools give you visibility into the health of your database, track query performance, and provide alerts when things are amiss. It's like having a health monitor for your database, ensuring it stays in tip-top shape. Monitoring can help you spot slow queries, replication issues, or resource bottlenecks before they escalate into full-blown disasters.

9. **Indexes** are the unsung heroes when it comes to managing large databases. They help MySQL locate data quickly, but just like superheroes, too many can lead to some unintended consequences. While indexes are fantastic for speeding up searches, they can slow down **INSERT**, **UPDATE**, and **DELETE** operations, as MySQL must update the indexes whenever data changes. So, like any good superhero, use indexes wisely and only on columns that will benefit from them. Regularly review your indexes to ensure they're still serving their purpose, and don't hesitate to remove unnecessary ones. Think of it like keeping your tools organized—too many can make a mess, but the right ones make all the difference.

10. **Data archiving** is a great way to manage large datasets without bogging down the main database. As data ages, it becomes less relevant for real-time queries but might still need to be stored for historical purposes. Archiving allows you to move older data to separate storage, reducing the load on your active database. You can use **partitioning** or **sharding** for archiving, or even store archived data in a different database or external storage like Amazon S3. For example, you can archive logs, old transactions, or historical records

that don't need to be queried frequently. It's like decluttering your house—keeping only the essentials in the living room, and storing the rest in the attic.

11. **Scaling your database** means balancing **read** and **write** operations. As your database grows, you'll likely face situations where the master server can't keep up with the load. One solution is to offload read queries to **replica** servers, allowing the master server to focus on write operations. This way, you can spread the load across multiple servers, ensuring that no single server becomes a bottleneck. Replication, which we discussed earlier, plays a key role in this setup. It's like having a team of assistants handling the paperwork while you focus on the important decisions—everything gets done more efficiently.

12. **Database normalization** plays a significant role in managing large databases, especially when dealing with complex relationships between data. Normalization helps reduce data redundancy and ensures that data is stored in the most efficient way possible. For example, instead of storing the same customer address in every order, you can store it in a separate `addresses` table and link it to the `orders` table via a foreign key. This reduces storage requirements and makes updates easier—if a customer moves, you only need to update their address in one place. However, too much normalization can lead to performance issues with complex joins. As with anything, balance is key—normalize where it makes sense, and denormalize when performance is critical.

13. **Replication lag** is a common issue when scaling large databases, particularly in **master-slave replication** setups. Replication lag occurs when the slave servers fall behind the master in applying changes, leading to stale data on the slaves. This can happen when the master is generating a high volume of transactions, or if the network connection between the master and slave is slow. To mitigate replication lag, you can monitor the **`Seconds_Behind_Master`** metric and optimize both the master and slave configurations. In extreme cases, you might want to consider upgrading hardware, using faster networks, or adding more slaves to distribute the load. It's like having a runner who can't keep up—sometimes, they need a little extra help to stay in the race.

14. **Concurrency control** is critical in large databases, especially when multiple transactions are running simultaneously. MySQL uses **InnoDB** as its default storage engine, which supports **row-level locking**. This ensures that two transactions can update different rows in the same table at the same time without blocking each other. However, deadlocks can still occur if two transactions try to update the same rows at the same time. MySQL can automatically detect deadlocks and roll back one of the transactions to resolve the issue. Deadlocks are like traffic jams—unavoidable at times, but with proper management, you can avoid long delays and keep the system flowing smoothly.

15. **Schema design** becomes even more important as your database grows. A well-designed schema can make it easier to scale and maintain your database, while a poorly designed schema can lead to performance issues, data inconsistencies, and maintenance headaches. When designing a schema for a large database, keep things modular by breaking data into logical tables with well-defined relationships. Use normalization to avoid redundancy, but

don't go overboard—too much normalization can lead to unnecessary complexity. Also, consider future growth—design your schema in a way that can handle increased data volumes without requiring a major redesign later. It's like building a house with expansion in mind—make sure the foundation is solid, but leave room for future additions.

16. **Data compression** can be a game-changer when managing large databases. Compressing data reduces storage requirements and can improve I/O performance by reducing the amount of data that needs to be read from disk. MySQL supports **COMPRESSED tables** with the **InnoDB** engine, which can automatically compress data to save space. For example, large text fields or logs can be compressed, reducing the overall size of your database without losing any data. However, compression can introduce overhead, so carefully measure its impact on read and write performance. It's like packing your clothes into a suitcase—squeeze them in without overpacking, and you'll save space.

17. **Query optimization** is an ongoing process, especially when managing large databases. You can start with the basics—**EXPLAIN** your queries, check for missing indexes, and avoid full-table scans. But as your database grows, you'll also need to optimize your server's configuration. Increase **`innodb_buffer_pool_size`** to allow InnoDB to cache more data in memory, reducing disk I/O. Adjust the **`query_cache_size`** to ensure MySQL isn't caching unnecessary queries. Also, regularly review your **slow query log** to identify queries that need optimization. Think of it like maintaining a car—you keep it running smoothly by tuning it up regularly and addressing any issues as they arise.

18. **Archiving old data** can also help manage large databases. As your database grows, some data becomes less relevant for day-to-day operations. By archiving old records to another table or storage system, you can keep your active database lean and responsive. For example, historical sales data or old transaction records can be moved to a separate archive database, reducing the size of the active database and improving query performance. Archiving is like cleaning out your closet—keeping only the clothes you actually wear and putting the rest in storage.

19. **Data consistency** is an ongoing challenge in large databases, especially when dealing with distributed systems or replication. To ensure consistency, consider using **ACID-compliant transactions** and **foreign keys** to enforce relationships between tables. MySQL's **InnoDB** engine supports full ACID compliance, meaning that transactions are guaranteed to be atomic, consistent, isolated, and durable. This ensures that your data remains consistent even in the event of failures or crashes. It's like making sure your bank account always reflects the correct balance, no matter how many transactions occur.

20. **Load balancing** becomes crucial as your database grows and you need to distribute queries across multiple servers. Load balancing ensures that no single server becomes overwhelmed by too many requests. You can use tools like **ProxySQL** or **HAProxy** to distribute traffic to the appropriate master or slave servers. Load balancing is like

assigning tasks to a group of people—you want to make sure everyone gets an equal share of the work so nobody gets overworked.

21. **Database security** becomes even more important as your database grows. A larger database often means more sensitive data, which makes it a bigger target for hackers. Use **role-based access control (RBAC)** to limit access to only the data that's necessary for each user. Encrypt sensitive data, both at rest and in transit, using SSL/TLS for communication between clients and the server. Regularly update MySQL and its dependencies to patch known vulnerabilities. Think of it like locking your doors and windows before going to bed—you want to make sure your database is safe from intruders.

22. **Data consistency and integrity** checks are essential as your database grows, especially when you have multiple replicas or distributed systems. Regularly check for **orphaned records**, missing foreign key constraints, or data discrepancies between the master and slave databases. MySQL offers **checksum** functions that allow you to verify the integrity of your data across servers. This ensures that your replication process hasn't introduced any corruption. It's like doing a routine inspection of your house—checking for leaks, cracks, or anything that could go wrong down the line.

23. **Horizontal scaling** becomes essential as your database grows beyond the capabilities of a single server. By **sharding** your data across multiple servers, you can distribute the load and handle more traffic. Sharding involves splitting data into separate databases or tables based on a key, such as customer ID or region. Each shard is stored on a different server, reducing the load on any single server. It's like spreading the workload across multiple employees so no one is overwhelmed.

24. **Backup strategies** are critical when managing large databases. With large datasets, backups can take longer, and restoring data can be a time-consuming process. Use **incremental backups** to back up only the data that has changed since the last backup. Consider setting up **offsite backups** for disaster recovery, ensuring that your data is safe even if the primary database server is compromised. Test your backup and recovery procedures regularly to make sure they work as expected. It's like practicing fire drills—you hope you never need them, but you'll be glad you have them when disaster strikes.

25. **Conclusion**: Managing large databases in MySQL requires a combination of the right strategies, tools, and best practices. From partitioning and sharding to query optimization and replication, there are many ways to ensure that your database can handle growth while staying fast and responsive. But it's not just about scaling your database—it's about maintaining its integrity, security, and consistency as it grows. With the right approach, you can turn your large MySQL database into a well-oiled machine that scales with ease and performs like a champion. So go ahead, scale up, and let your database handle the heavy lifting—because when you know how to manage it, even the largest database can feel like a breeze.

Chapter 25: Mastering MySQL: Future Trends and Beyond

1. Congratulations! You've made it through the complexities of MySQL and emerged with a solid understanding of how to tame even the largest, most demanding databases. But the world of databases is always evolving, and there's no stopping the constant **innovation** in the field. This chapter is all about looking into the future of MySQL—where it's headed, what's new on the horizon, and how you can stay ahead of the curve. Think of this as your crystal ball, showing you the trends that will shape MySQL for years to come. From cloud-native databases to machine learning integration, there's no shortage of exciting developments. So, put on your time-traveling hat, because we're about to explore the future of MySQL and what's next for those who want to master it.

2. **Cloud-native MySQL** is already gaining traction, and it's only going to become more important in the future. With cloud infrastructure becoming the norm, many organizations are shifting their databases to the cloud to take advantage of **scalability**, **flexibility**, and **cost-effectiveness**. MySQL can now run natively on cloud platforms like **Amazon RDS**, **Google Cloud SQL**, and **Azure Database for MySQL**, providing a managed service that reduces the operational burden. It's like hiring a personal assistant who handles the boring stuff, so you can focus on the big picture. Cloud-native MySQL services allow for automatic scaling, automatic backups, and high availability, making it easier to scale your database without worrying about the underlying infrastructure. In the future, we'll likely see **even more seamless integration** with cloud-native technologies like Kubernetes, allowing MySQL to be containerized and deployed with ease. The cloud is the future—just don't forget to keep your cloud bill under control!

3. **Serverless MySQL** is a future trend that takes cloud-native databases a step further. Imagine running your MySQL database without ever having to worry about provisioning or managing servers. With serverless databases, your MySQL instance scales up and down automatically based on usage, without any manual intervention. For example, AWS **Aurora Serverless** allows you to pay only for the actual usage of your database, rather than maintaining a constantly running instance. Serverless databases are perfect for workloads with unpredictable traffic or low-to-moderate usage, such as small apps, startups, or projects with **seasonal** spikes. It's like having an elastic database that adapts to your needs—expand it when traffic peaks, and shrink it back down when things slow down. As serverless technology matures, we can expect MySQL to become even more adaptable and efficient, reducing operational overhead for developers.

4. **MySQL on Kubernetes** is the future of managing MySQL in **containerized** environments. Kubernetes is becoming the de facto standard for container orchestration, and MySQL is no stranger to this trend. By running MySQL in Kubernetes clusters, you can enjoy all the benefits of containerization: portability, scalability, and easy deployment. Kubernetes allows for **auto-scaling** of MySQL pods based on load, so you won't need to worry about provisioning new servers manually. It's like being able to deploy and scale your database as easily as clicking a button—no more manually configuring servers or adjusting settings. As container orchestration tools like Kubernetes continue to evolve, we'll see better integration with MySQL, including built-in high availability, fault tolerance, and seamless updates. Running MySQL on Kubernetes will be an essential skill for modern database administrators in the future.

5. **Multi-cloud and hybrid cloud** setups are on the rise, and they will likely play a bigger role in MySQL's future. Organizations are moving away from relying on a single cloud provider and are adopting **multi-cloud** or **hybrid-cloud** strategies to increase **resilience**, **avoid vendor lock-in**, and leverage the best features of different cloud providers. With MySQL, this means running your database across multiple cloud platforms (like AWS, Google Cloud, and Azure), providing flexibility and minimizing the risk of outages. The key to managing MySQL in multi-cloud environments is ensuring data consistency and high availability across platforms, and with the right setup, MySQL can handle this seamlessly. Think of it as having multiple safety nets, just in case one falls through. In the future, expect MySQL to offer even better support for multi-cloud configurations, enabling **easy failover** and **load balancing** across different cloud providers.

6. **Distributed MySQL databases** are also gaining traction, especially as organizations look to scale globally. Instead of having one monolithic database that serves all traffic, **distributed databases** spread data across multiple nodes and locations. This helps reduce latency and improve performance for users in different regions of the world. MySQL's **Group Replication** and **NDB Cluster** are examples of technologies that allow MySQL to operate in a distributed fashion. Group Replication helps achieve fault tolerance and high availability by ensuring that all replicas are synchronized, while NDB Cluster offers **shared-nothing architecture** for horizontal scalability. The future of MySQL is distributed, with better support for **sharding**, **replication**, and **geo-distributed databases**. This is like having multiple small stores in different cities, each serving its local customers quickly, while still being part of a larger brand.

7. **Machine learning and AI integration** are not just buzzwords—they're becoming increasingly important in database management. As machine learning and artificial intelligence continue to reshape industries, MySQL will likely see deeper integration with these technologies to help with **query optimization**, **anomaly detection**, and **predictive maintenance**. Imagine a MySQL database that can automatically detect slow queries and suggest indexes or changes to improve performance. AI-powered systems could also predict future database growth and automatically scale MySQL resources to meet demand before it becomes a problem. It's like having a personal assistant who doesn't just schedule your meetings but also helps you make decisions based on data and trends. The integration of **machine learning models** into MySQL is just beginning, and in the future, we'll likely see tools that allow MySQL to optimize itself based on **real-time usage patterns**.

8. **MySQL in the world of Big Data** will evolve as well. Big Data technologies like **Apache Hadoop**, **Apache Spark**, and **NoSQL databases** are popular for handling large-scale, unstructured data. However, MySQL isn't going anywhere—it's adapting and integrating with these technologies. With tools like **MySQL Fabric** and **MySQL Cluster**, MySQL is increasingly being used in **Big Data environments** to handle structured transactional data alongside unstructured data. In the future, MySQL will likely continue to bridge the gap between relational databases and NoSQL technologies, making it easier for organizations to manage diverse data types. It's like being able to

host both your traditional company records and the piles of **big data** without running into confusion or inefficiency.

9. **Automated Database Tuning** is something that MySQL is moving toward, making it easier to fine-tune your database for peak performance. We all know that tuning a MySQL server requires an intimate understanding of **buffer sizes**, **query cache settings**, **thread concurrency**, and a whole host of other parameters. In the future, MySQL will likely offer automated tuning options that analyze workloads and automatically adjust configurations to optimize performance. Think of it as an autopilot for your MySQL database, adjusting the speed and settings to match the traffic. With **machine learning** and **adaptive algorithms**, MySQL will be able to analyze traffic patterns and continuously optimize itself without requiring constant human intervention.

10. **Serverless databases** are the wave of the future, and MySQL is jumping on board with services like **Aurora Serverless**. In serverless environments, the database automatically scales up and down based on traffic demand, without the need to manually provision or manage servers. This flexibility will allow MySQL to seamlessly handle **spiky workloads**, where traffic fluctuates unpredictably, without the need for intervention. Serverless databases also reduce costs, as you only pay for the resources you actually use. It's like renting a database that expands when you have lots of guests and contracts when you're not entertaining. Serverless MySQL will allow organizations to focus on development without worrying about the underlying infrastructure.

11. **Improved JSON support** will be a major trend in MySQL, especially as **unstructured data** continues to become more prevalent. While MySQL already supports JSON as a data type, future versions will offer even more powerful tools for working with JSON data. You can already use functions like `JSON_EXTRACT()` and `JSON_SET()` to query and manipulate JSON data, but expect to see **enhanced indexing** and **searching capabilities** for JSON fields, making it easier to work with this format at scale. As more applications deal with JSON-heavy data (think **logs**, **configuration files**, and **web data**), MySQL will likely continue to improve its **performance** and **functionality** for handling JSON. It's like turning your database into a **JSON ninja**, able to slice through complex data structures with ease.

12. **Security** will continue to be a major focus for MySQL in the future. With data breaches and cyberattacks on the rise, MySQL will keep improving its **encryption**, **authentication**, and **access control** features to ensure that your database is protected from unauthorized access. Expect to see stronger **role-based access control (RBAC)**, **multi-factor authentication (MFA)**, and **encrypted backups** as part of MySQL's evolving security model. Future versions may also offer **intrusion detection systems** that automatically flag suspicious queries or actions. Just as you lock your doors at night, you'll want to make sure your MySQL database is locked down and safe from prying eyes.

Hybrid cloud database deployments will become increasingly common as organizations seek to balance flexibility and control. Many companies will opt for hybrid solutions, where their

MySQL database runs both on-premises and in the cloud, giving them the ability to leverage both environments. This setup allows organizations to keep sensitive data on-premises while taking advantage of the cloud's scalability for less sensitive operations. MySQL will likely offer better support for hybrid environments, making it easier to integrate your on-premise databases with cloud infrastructure seamlessly. It's like having the best of both worlds—keeping your most critical data secure on your premises while letting the cloud handle the scaling and flexibility.

Data privacy regulations like GDPR and CCPA are becoming increasingly important, and MySQL will need to continue evolving to ensure compliance. With the tightening of data protection laws, database administrators will need to ensure that they're handling personal data securely. MySQL will likely provide enhanced features to help with **data anonymization**, **encryption**, and **audit logs** to make compliance easier. The future of MySQL will likely see **built-in tools** that help automate privacy features, like automatically encrypting personal information or flagging data that falls under privacy regulations. Think of it as MySQL becoming the compliance officer—ensuring you're always within the legal lines.

Multi-version concurrency control (**MVCC**) will continue to improve in MySQL, especially in the context of managing large-scale databases. MVCC is a method of concurrency control that allows multiple transactions to access the same data without interfering with each other. MySQL already supports MVCC with its **InnoDB** storage engine, but as databases grow larger, we can expect improvements in how MVCC handles **high-concurrency scenarios**. These improvements will make MySQL even more capable of handling millions of transactions simultaneously, ensuring that your database remains **consistent** and **efficient** even during peak times. It's like running a busy restaurant with multiple chefs—everyone can work without stepping on each other's toes.

Enhanced indexing techniques will be critical as MySQL continues to scale. While traditional B-tree indexes are great, we'll see more sophisticated indexing methods designed to handle the massive datasets of the future. **Bitmap indexes**, **full-text indexes**, and **spatial indexes** will evolve to better handle the growing complexities of modern data. MySQL will likely introduce **dynamic indexing**, where indexes automatically adjust based on query patterns and data changes, making indexing more efficient and less resource-intensive. This is like turning your database into a smart index that learns and adapts over time, optimizing its own structure.

Graph databases and **MySQL** may become more integrated as graph data modeling grows in importance. While MySQL is excellent for structured relational data, the rise of social networks, recommendation systems, and IoT has driven the need for **graph-based queries** that connect different entities in complex ways. MySQL may offer better support for **graph databases**, either by integrating with external graph database tools or introducing native graph query functionality. Imagine using MySQL not only to store data but to intuitively understand the relationships between various pieces of information, like social media connections or interconnected devices. This integration could bring **SQL and graph models** together, offering you the best of both worlds.

AI-driven performance optimization is another exciting development on the horizon. As machine learning and AI technologies continue to advance, MySQL will likely incorporate these technologies into **query optimization**, **index management**, and **automated troubleshooting**.

Imagine your database monitoring system being able to automatically **learn** from previous performance issues and proactively suggest optimizations or configurations. This would reduce the need for human intervention, freeing up your time to focus on more strategic tasks. It's like having a personal assistant who understands how your database works and fixes issues before they even become problems.

MySQL on ARM-based architecture is something to watch, especially as **cloud providers** and **on-premise systems** shift toward ARM processors for performance and efficiency. ARM-based chips are known for being energy-efficient while still providing impressive computational power. In the future, MySQL will likely offer **optimized performance** for ARM-based servers, allowing you to take advantage of these more **cost-effective** and **environmentally friendly** hardware solutions. This could make running large-scale MySQL instances much more affordable, especially for companies looking to cut down on power consumption while still maintaining performance. It's like upgrading your system to a high-performance engine that also runs on less fuel—saving you money and reducing your carbon footprint.

Support for JSON and NoSQL-like features will continue to evolve. As MySQL becomes more flexible, expect it to include better integration with **NoSQL capabilities** and **document-based models**. With more applications requiring schema-less data storage, MySQL will continue to enhance its **JSON functions**, allowing for even more efficient querying and indexing of JSON data. This means that MySQL could become even better at handling semi-structured or unstructured data, making it a more versatile tool for a wide range of applications. It's like turning MySQL into a hybrid—one part relational database, one part NoSQL database, all seamlessly integrated.

Decentralized database management is another trend that may emerge as MySQL adapts to the rise of **blockchain** and **distributed ledger technologies**. As these technologies become more mainstream, there will be a growing need for databases that can handle decentralized and immutable data. MySQL may evolve to support **blockchain-like features**, allowing for the easy storage and management of tamper-proof data. Imagine using MySQL to track **supply chains**, **financial transactions**, or **digital assets** in a decentralized network. While MySQL is currently built for traditional database setups, future versions could integrate seamlessly with blockchain and decentralized networks, unlocking new possibilities for secure, transparent data management.

Automatic failover and high availability will continue to improve, with MySQL embracing **self-healing clusters**. The days of manually switching over to a backup server during downtime will be replaced by automated systems that detect failures and recover within seconds. **Group Replication** and **InnoDB Cluster** are already laying the groundwork for this, but expect MySQL to further refine these tools. Imagine your MySQL cluster automatically diagnosing a failure, fixing the issue, and getting your data back up and running without any manual intervention. It's like having a team of highly trained medical professionals who can heal themselves—ready to tackle any problem that arises.

Database as a service (DBaaS) will continue to rise, and MySQL will be at the forefront of this revolution. Many companies are shifting away from managing their own infrastructure and are moving toward DBaaS platforms that take care of the **back-end** operations. These platforms handle everything from database provisioning and maintenance to scaling and backups, allowing developers to focus solely on their applications. MySQL will become even more tightly integrated with cloud providers, offering **out-of-the-box solutions** for developers who want to eliminate the operational overhead. This trend will drive MySQL to continue improving its **managed service offerings**, making it easier than ever to deploy and manage MySQL databases in the cloud.

Edge computing and MySQL will play a growing role in the future, especially as the demand for **real-time data** increases. With **IoT devices**, **smart cities**, and **edge-based applications** becoming more popular, there's a greater need for databases that can store and process data at the edge of the network. MySQL will likely evolve to support **distributed database setups** at the edge, where it can run on local servers or devices close to the data source. This will allow for faster processing and lower latency, especially for applications that require real-time insights. It's like having a **mini-database** on every street corner, capable of making instant decisions without relying on a distant server.

The future of MySQL is incredibly exciting, with new features and innovations on the horizon that will make it even more powerful, scalable, and adaptable. From AI-driven optimization to better cloud integration, MySQL is continually evolving to meet the demands of the modern world. As database administrators, developers, and system architects, we need to stay ahead of these trends and adopt the technologies that will help us build **better, faster, and more reliable databases**. Whether you're scaling to massive proportions, embracing the cloud, or exploring new types of data storage, MySQL will be there, evolving with you every step of the way. So, while we've covered the basics and the advanced features of MySQL, remember that the journey doesn't stop here. The future is bright, and MySQL is ready for the next big thing.

www.ingramcontent.com/pod-product-compliance
Lightning Source LLC
LaVergne TN
LVHW080117070326
832902LV00015B/2634